The Power of Prophecy

Rev. Wallace H. Heflin

Published by:

The McDougal Publishing Company
P.O. Box 3595
Hagerstown, MD 21742-3595

ISBN 1-884369-22-7

Printed in the United States of America
For worldwide distribution

For personal correspondence with the author, write:
11352 Heflin Lane, Ashland, Virginia, 23005.

Dedication

I dedicate this book to my mother (who will be 85 on November 4, 1995), for her example to us all in the realm of prophecy. The revival of the latter part of the 1940s, a revival which coincided with the formation of the nation of Israel, gave birth to new gifts and ministries in her life, and the most dynamic of these was prophecy.

For many years she stood as an example and a challenge to all of us, as she poured herself out to hungry souls wherever they could be found. She has been a 'real trooper,' and we are grateful to God for her and humbly recognize that we are where we are today because of her faithfulness.

She still enjoys sitting in the glory.

Other books by Rev. Wallace H. Heflin:

A Pocket Full of Miracles:
> The story of Calvary Pentecostal Campground in Ashland, Virginia.

Power In Your Hand:
> The secrets of God doing everyday miracles through everyday people like YOU.
> *(Available also in Spanish)*

The Potter's House:
> The steps the Master Potter takes to make and perfect a vessel fit for His service.

Jacob and Esau, Birthright and Blessing:
> The truth about the birthright and the blessing and how you can have them today.

The Bride:
> Identification of and exhortation to the Bride that time is short and that her marriage to the Lamb will soon be consummated.

Contents

The hand of the Lord was upon me, and carried me out in the spirit of the Lord, and set me down in the midst of the valley which was full of bones, And caused me to pass by them round about: and, behold, there were very many in the open valley; and, lo, they were very dry. And he said unto me, Son of man, can these bones live? and I answered, O Lord God, thou knowest.

Again he said unto me, Prophesy upon these bones, and say unto them, O ye dry bones, hear the word of the Lord. Thus saith the Lord God unto these bones; Behold, I will cause breath to enter into you, and ye shall live: And I will lay sinews upon you, and will bring up flesh upon you, and cover you with skin, and put breath in you, and ye shall live; and ye shall know that I am the Lord.

So I prophesied as I was commanded: and as I prophesied, there was a noise, and behold a shaking, and the bones came together, bone to his bone. And when I beheld, lo, the sinews and the flesh came up upon them, and the skin covered them above: but there was no breath in them.

Then said he unto me, Prophesy unto the wind, prophesy, son of man, and say to the wind, Thus saith the Lord God; Come from the four winds, O breath, and breathe upon these slain, that they may live. So I prophesied as he commanded me, and the breath came into them, and they lived, and stood up upon their feet, an exceeding great army.

Then he said unto me, Son of man, these bones are the whole house of Israel: behold, they say, Our bones are dried, and our hope is lost: we are cut off for our parts. Therefore prophesy and say unto them, Thus saith the Lord God; Behold, O my people, I will open your graves, and cause you to come up out of your graves, and bring you into the land of Israel. And ye shall know that I am the Lord, when I have opened your graves, O My people, and brought you up out of your graves, And shall put my spirit in you, and ye shall live, and I shall place you in your own land: then shall ye know that I the Lord have spoken it, and performed it, saith the Lord.

Ezekiel 37:1-12

Introduction

Of all the nine gifts of the Spirit, prophecy is the one that God is using the most to bring in the revival of the end-time. And, because of that, prophecy is being opposed now more than any other gift of the Spirit. Common arguments are that prophecy was only for the Old Testament period and is no longer needed, that prophecy is limited in its application, or that prophecy can be exercised by only a few chosen people.

I want to declare that it is time to take the limits off of the gift of prophecy and off of the prophets God has raised up for this hour. It is time to move into God's plan of action to declare His will prophetically to this, the final generation. Men and women desperately need to hear from Heaven, and we, as spirit-filled Christians, have the means available to us to allow our generation to know the will and mind of God right now. We must not hold back.

I was not always so deeply committed to the ministry of prophecy. In fact, I was more interested in the gift of healing for many years. After I came to know the Lord, I was so impressed with the ministry of my father in this regard, that I asked God to give me a ministry just like his.

He was a man of great faith who was used by God to bring healing to many difficult cases. And the healings that resulted from his simple prayers of faith opened doors of opportunity to him and made him successful in the ministry. He was known up and down the eastern seaboard as a man that God used in this unusual way and was invited to speak in conventions in many parts of the country because of it.

The churches we have in the State of Virginia are churches my father pioneered through his tent ministry and the miracles of healing God gave him in those meetings. For a period he belonged to an organization of more than three thousand ministers in which he was bishop over twelve states. His ministry of healing brought great respect to his life.

I decided that I wanted that same miracle ministry and began to fast and pray for God to give it to me. For many weeks, I fasted six days during the week, ate on Sunday, and then resumed my fast for the next six days. I continued this until God began to do in my life the same thing He was doing in my father's ministry.

The ministry of my mother was quite different, and I respected her for it. She was a teacher, but she also had a unique gift of prophecy, very unusual for her time. When she had finished teaching she would begin to pray for people and God would give her a word for individuals, many of whom she was seeing for the first time, and the word she gave would often turn their lives around.

I was so moved by her gift that I often stood beside her in the morning services of our campmeeting and watched what was happening. I was amazed, first of all, at how far people had come just to receive her prayer. We often received calls from people asking if Mother would be ministering in the morning service. They didn't ask, "Will your mother be prophesying?" But I knew what was compelling them to come. If she was ministering, they would fly in for the day or for a weekend or longer and stand in line to have her hands laid on them.

I had the opportunity to greet many of those same people as they came onto the campground, and I couldn't help but notice that some were discouraged, despondent and lacking direction in their lives. They knew that they needed to hear from God. They needed clarity of thought. They needed God's assurance that everything was going to be all right.

Then, as Mother laid hands on them and ministered to them through the Spirit, I watched as their lives were transformed before my eyes. Some of those who came for prayer were sinners, but they didn't remain sinners long under her touch. And those who came in search of direction for their lives and ministries left with new and clear direction. In fact, very respected ministers often came just to get God's direction for an important decision they had to make.

I was, in fact, so stirred by the results of Mother's ministry that I began to pray, "God, give me a ministry just like my mother's." This is a biblical prayer, for God said:

Covet earnestly the best gifts.
1 Corinthians 12:31

All the gifts and ministries of the Spirit are so wonderful that we have always hesitated to name one as being more wonderful than another. I believe, however, that *the best gifts* are those that are needed at the particular moment and those that can best bring glory to God. And, I have come to the conclusion that prophecy is the gift of the hour.

Later, in chapter 14, Paul specifically exhorted the Church:

Covet to prophesy.   1 Corinthians 14:39

The word *covet,* as used in both these verses denotes *a strong desire,* a moving desire. It was just such *a strong desire* that caused God to answer my prayer and to give me the ministry of prophecy. And through that ministry I have seen lives changed on every continent.

I trust that the message of this book will bring *a strong desire* to your heart and life, a desire to be used for God's glory in these final days of time, a desire to be a voice for God in our chaotic world, a desire to bring hope and enlightenment to our present generation. This is my prayer.

Rev. Wallace Heflin
Ashland, Virginia

Part I

Fundamentals of
New Testament Prophecy

- 1 -

What Is Prophecy?

Because prophecy is not commonly accepted and practiced by a majority of our modern churches, there exists a whole host of inaccurate teachings about what it really is. So we need to begin by seeing just what we mean by *prophecy*. It might help us to begin by seeing what prophecy is not.

What Prophecy Is Not

In several of our modern language English translations of the Bible, the word *prophecy* is translated as *preaching*. Let me begin by saying that prophecy is not preaching. While it is good for parts of our preaching to be prophetic in nature, that is of instantaneous inspiration, it is wrong to say that prophecy is preaching.

For the most part, we preach what we have learned and experienced over a period of years. Prophecy, on the other hand, is a totally spontaneous speaking out of that which we have not previously rehearsed and may indeed be that which we have neither learned nor experienced. In prophecy, the person speaking is responding to the inspiration of the Spirit of God.

Some people quote scripture or read from the Bible in a service, thinking that this is a substitute for prophecy. It isn't! The Bible is the revelation of the will and plan of God. God also wants to speak to every one of us and give us more detailed direction for our lives. While God does speak to us through His written Word, prophecy is different and should not be confused with Bible reading.

When some people think of prophecy, they think only of predicting the future. Prophecy, however, is not limited to predicting the future and may have to do with the past, the present or the future. A general guideline for the purpose of prophecy is found in Paul's teachings to the Corinthians. He said:

> *But he that prophesieth speaketh unto men to edification, exhortation, and comfort.*
> 1 Corinthians 14:4

The purpose of prophecy is not to expose people's sins or to divulge hidden things in public. It is not a tool of public rebuke. If your sins are covered by the blood of Jesus, you can rest assured that God will never reveal them. In fact, He doesn't even remember them anymore.

Prophecy is not your way of challenging others. It is not your way of getting across a point of view. It is not a means of speaking out some difference you have with a brother or sister that you are afraid or ashamed to speak with them about in private.

Prophecy is not a tool of personal vindictiveness. It is not something you think of at home that you believe needs to be said in the service. Prophecy is from God, and we prophesy exactly what He gives us to say, nothing more and nothing less.

What Prophecy Is

Prophecy is a message from God given in a spontaneous way through an individual who yields himself or herself to God for this purpose. It is one of the nine gifts of the Spirit placed by God in the Church for its edification. Prophecy, along with the gifts of tongues and interpretation of tongues, has been called an "inspirational" gift, and that has a dual meaning. What is spoken in prophecy is inspired of God, and when it is spoken it inspires the hearers.

Prophecy is nothing new. It has always existed. In fact, all of the gifts of the Spirit are evident in the Old Testament, except speaking in tongues and the interpretation of tongues. God has always had those who spoke on His behalf.

Some of the Old Testament prophets were so famous that most of us recognize their names immediately: Samuel, Elijah and Elisha, Isaiah and

Jeremiah, Jonah and Malachi. There were many others, and their words were deemed to be so divinely inspired that they were accepted as part of our sacred texts, the Bible.

Of the Old Testament brand of prophecy, Peter declared:

> *For the prophecy came not in old time by the will of man: but holy men of God spake as they were moved by the Holy Ghost.*   2 Peter 1:21

In this regard, New Testament prophets differ little from their Old Testament counterparts. They are persons *moved by the Holy Ghost,* and their words are also divinely inspired. In fact the written Word of God and the spoken word have many things in common.

The written Word of God is likened to a two-edged sword, one which cuts both coming and going:

> *For the word of God is quick, and powerful, and sharper than any twoedged sword, piercing even to the dividing asunder of soul and spirit, and of the joints and marrow, and is a discerner of the thoughts and intents of the heart.*
> Hebrews 4:12

This is true of the prophetic word also and is the reason Paul could write to the Corinthians:

> *But if all prophesy, and there come in one that believeth not, or one unlearned, he is convinced*

of all, he is judged of all: And thus are the secrets of his heart made manifest; and so falling down on his face he will worship God, and report that God is in you of a truth.
                                    1 Corinthians 14:24-25

The written Word of God is described as a hammer.

Is not my word like ... a hammer that breaketh the rock in pieces?   Jeremiah 23:29

In the same way, the prophetic word of the Lord is able to break stony hearts and soften them to receive His goodness.

Jesus was Himself a prophet and the Prophet of Prophets. The words that He spoke while He was on the earth, which also came to form part of the Bible, were described as *spirit and ... life.*

It is the spirit that quickeneth; the flesh profiteth nothing: the words that I speak unto you, they are spirit, and they are life.   John 6:63

In the same way, the prophetic word can bring life into the individual who hears it with an open heart. Death turns to life when the creative word is declared and when the person receiving that word responds positively to what God is saying.

The written Word of God never *returns void.*

So shall my word be that goeth forth out of my mouth: it shall not return unto me void, but it shall accomplish that which I please, and it shall prosper in the thing whereto I sent it.

Isaiah 55:11

It shall not return void.
It shall accomplish that which I please.
It shall prosper.

Since prophetic utterances are inspired of God, they are *words that go forth out of [His] mouth.* Therefore, they fall under these same promises. Words that are inspired by God cannot fail. Therefore, a person who is hearing from God and is faithfully speaking forth what God is saying, can rest assured that what he says will indeed prosper. It cannot fail.

Of the written Word, Jesus said:

Heaven and earth shall pass away, but my words shall not pass away.   Matthew 24:35

And the prophetic word from God is just as reliable. Because it is from God and not man, we can rely on it.

The personality involved in prophecy, the prophet, is not the center of attention. John the Baptist was a prophet of God and refused to take any credit for the blessings that flowed from his words. He said, *I am [just] the voice*:

I am the voice of one crying in the wilderness, Make straight the way of the Lord, as said the prophet Esaias. John 1:23

Prophecy is a message from God. He is the Source. We are just the *voices* that bring that message forth to those that He indicates.

The Bible offers a definition of prophecy. It says:

The testimony of Jesus is the spirit of prophecy. Revelation 19:10

Prophecy, then, is Jesus speaking to our hearts. That is why it is edifying. That is why it is a model of exhortation. That is why it is comforting.

When Jesus came to the earth to speak personally with man, the Devil tried every way he could to stop Him. And Satan will try everything in his power to prevent prophecy from coming forth in the Church today because he doesn't want us to hear from Jesus.

David's inspired 19th Psalm speaks of *the testimony of the Lord* (the spirit of prophecy) *making wise the simple:*

The testimony of the Lord is sure, making wise the simple. Psalms 19:7

If there was ever a time in which the Church needed to hear from Heaven, it is today. Many of those who are pastoring our spiritual flocks are still preaching and teaching the same things they were preaching and teaching several years ago. They have nothing new and fresh to offer. Yet, God always has something fresh and new for us. If we will let the Spirit of God move upon us, we can bring forth a fresh word to every weary man and woman and see their lives turned around.

Feeding the Flock

In many churches, we pray only for those who have apparent needs. We invite the sinners to be saved, and many are saved. We invite the sick to be healed, and many are healed. We invite those who are hungry for God's Spirit to be filled, and many are filled.

But once you have been saved, and healed, and filled with the Spirit, most churches have nothing more to offer you, it seems, and they rarely or never minister to the rest of the congregation.

This is a tragedy, for every believer needs to maintain life so that they can go out and produce sheep. Every believer needs direction in his or her daily walk with God. Every believer needs encouragement at some point of severe trial. And every believer needs to be edified, exhorted and comforted.

We need prophecy today just as much or more than God's people have needed it throughout the centuries. A single prophecy, given under the anointing of the Spirit of God, can turn a service around and give it new direction, new impetus, and new anointing and a single anointed prophecy can change the life of every believer.

Many of us are saved or healed or filled with the Holy Ghost today because someone obeyed God and spoke forth the promise of what God had for us in a service we attended. Let us return the favor to others.

God is looking for men and women who will get out of the rut, out of the pattern of things we have been walking in now for some time, and take a new step in the Spirit. God is looking for men and women who will be willing to be thought foolish for God in order to bring new life into existing situations.

Being conservative is comfortable, and most churches prefer not to take chances. They feel safe with the familiar. Some churches have trained their deacons to approach anyone who does anything out of the ordinary and quietly pray for them or lead them out of the service, if necessary. They don't feel comfortable with the unusual.

But our God is a God of variety. He delights in moving in a variety of ways. He desires to have pre-eminence in every service, to do things in His way and to, thus, receive all the glory for everything that is accomplished. He has many new things to offer His people in these days.

Don't be afraid of the new. Don't be afraid of the different. If something is always the same, it may mean that it has stopped growing, and that's danger-ous. Let God do a new thing in your life. Let Him use you to bring forth His prophetic promises.

Prophecy is important to the Church today because God has greater things in store for us than we can ever imagine. He wants higher things for us than we want for ourselves. He can do far more than we can even *ask or think.*

> *Now unto him that is able to do exceeding abundantly above all that we ask or think, according to the power that worketh in us,*
> Ephesians 3:20

Let that power work in you. Let your spirit be stirred to lay aside the old habits and to take on a new challenge, to become a voice for God in this present age.

Is Prophecy Only A Confirming Word?

Many are teaching that New Testament prophecy serves only as a confirming word, and they don't want to receive a prophecy that seems to be an initiating word, but they are wrong. We cannot limit God in this way.

"If this is of God," they say, "why didn't God tell me personally?" Many times, because of our circumstances, we have difficulty seeing something that God is trying to show us. Someone else, free from those constraints, may see more clearly what God's will is at that moment. If a prophet is listening and you are not, or if the prophet is moving in a greater level of faith than you are, that person may have something important to say to you. The prophet's realm of faith and his experience in God makes him know that what he is hearing from heaven can be done and will be done, if you will believe it and act on it. The prophet, therefore, often speaks beyond your faith to let you know what the future holds for you as you obey and grow in God.

And God has set such people of faith and experience in the Church. The office of prophet is one of those listed by Paul as being among the most basic of New Testament ministries, placed by God in the Church *for the perfecting of the saints.*

> *And he gave some, apostles; and some, prophets; and some, evangelists; and some, pastors and teachers; For the perfecting of the saints, for the work of the ministry, for the edifying of the body of Christ: Till we all come in the unity of the faith, and of the knowledge of the Son of God, unto a perfect man, unto the measure of the stature of the fulness of Christ: That we henceforth be no more children, tossed to and fro, and carried about with every wind of doctrine, by the sleight of men, and cunning craftiness, whereby they lie in wait to deceive;*
>
> Ephesians 4:11-14

The ministry of the prophet is just as valid and important to the church today as the ministry of the pastor and the ministry of the teacher. Thank God that He loves us enough to speak to us through others. He has said in His Word:

> *Believe in the Lord your God, so shall ye be established; believe his prophets, so shall ye prosper.*   2 Chronicles 20:20
> *Should ye not hear the words which the Lord hath cried by the ... prophets ... ?*
>   Zechariah 7:7

So, although God speaks to each of His children, He has placed prophets among us, men and women who have an ear to hear the voice of God and who are able to bring us a word which we might not receive in any other way. Because of this, it is a mistake to say that prophecy is only a confirming word.

Indeed, God has declared that He does nothing without first showing His prophets:

> *Surely the Lord God will do nothing, but he revealeth his secret unto his servants the prophets.*   Amos 3:7

If you are hearing the voice of God for yourself, prophecy *is* often a confirming word. But it can also be used to tell you something you have never heard before. Usually this comes when the word is given by a more spiritually mature person who has a greater depth and insight into the heart of God. It may, however, come from the simplest child or childlike believer, and we should respect it just as much when it comes in that way.

Paul was not offended when the prophet Agabus spoke of how the apostle would be bound in Jerusalem. Paul didn't argue that he could hear from God himself and, therefore, didn't need the help of Agabus.

> *And as we tarried there many days, there came down from Judaea a certain prophet, named Agabus. And when he was come unto us, he took Paul's girdle, and bound his own hands and feet, and said, Thus saith the Holy Ghost, So shall the Jews at Jerusalem bind the man that owneth this girdle, and shall deliver him into the hands of the Gentiles.*   Acts 21:10-11

In the same way, Paul was not offended when he received a word from the daughters of Philip. He did not respond that it was not proper for such young ladies to be giving a word to such a mature man of God.

> *And the next day we that were of Paul's company departed, and came unto Caesarea: and we entered into the house of Philip the evangelist, which was one of the seven; and abode with him. And the same man had four daughters, virgins, which did prophesy.*   Acts 21:8-9

Whether prophecy is a confirming word or an initiating word doesn't matter. If God speaks to us, we should act on what He is telling us — regardless of the message and regardless of the person God is using to give us the message.

Yes, we take more seriously the message of mature people. That is understandable. When a person is more mature, they have more depth of vision and, therefore, should be able to give us better spiritual counsel. But is not necessarily so. God uses the Davids, the Gideons and the Deborahs of this world (ordinary people until God raises them up) to confound the wise.

God desires to speak to His people, both individually and corporately, and has placed the gift of prophecy and the ministry of the prophet in the church for this purpose. When individuals are edified through personal prophecy, the whole church is edified. Let Him speak!

He has said:

> *He that prophesieth edifieth the church.*
> 1 Corinthians 14:4

If there were no other verse in the Bible about prophecy, this one would be enough. Prophecy edifies (builds up) the Church. What else needs to be said?

What Does Prophecy Accomplish?

What is the effect of prophecy? What does it produce? What does it accomplish? If it does nothing, then we are not interested in it. If, however, it can change our lives, we want it, and we want it now. Realizing the benefits of prophecy can make us hungry to receive it.

A few examples of the effectiveness of prophecy upon various servants of God immediately come to mind:

Examples

A preacher went out of his way to come to my tent meeting in Roanoke, Virginia, to tell what God had done for him through the prophetic word. I had prophesied over him in summer campmeeting in Ashland, Virginia. He had felt so hopeless about his situation. Nothing seemed to be happening in his ministry. But when he went back home, God increased the size of his church and blessed him financially so that he was able to buy both a van and a bus for traveling ministry. He was so excited that he came all the way to the tent to praise God publicly for His goodness.

A pastor in North Carolina was so discouraged that he was ready to give up his church and leave town. He had already told his church overseer that he insisted on being relocated because nothing was going well for him where he was. He attended our tent meeting, and I ministered to him in prophecy. Later, some of the members of his church came to thank me. He was so changed, they said, that it was like having a new pastor. They were grateful and so was he.

After a few months, I got a letter from him. "My whole church is turned upside down," he wrote. "I thought we loved God and were worshiping God, but I wonder what we were doing all those years. My life has been totally changed." His overseer had found another church for him, but he refused it and said that he would not leave town for all the money in the world — because God was moving and working in his congregation.

People come to our campmeeting from all over the world, and many Nigerian ministers come. I receive letters from many of them later telling how their situation has been turned around for the glory of God because of a word they received at the camp.

God told one Nigerian brother that he would soon be elevated. When he returned home, he was elected president of a Pentecostal association of churches. He wrote me to give the Lord thanks.

A couple traveled from Iceland to attend the camp. One day God spoke to them in great detail through prophecy. He showed them that He knew all about their problems at home and that He had something great in mind for them. They were slain in the Spirit on the floor of the Tabernacle and got up a while later with a totally new lease on life.

What does prophecy accomplish? It accomplishes very much!

Prophecy Brings Enlightenment

God has shown us that He does not want us to be *ignorant,* to be caught off guard, to walk blindly into some dangerous situation, or to ever be without the knowledge we need in a given situation:

> *Now I would not have you ignorant, brethren, that ... .* Romans 1:13

> *For I would not, brethren, that ye should be ignorant of this mystery ... .* Romans 11:25

> *Moreover, brethren, I would not that ye should be ignorant, how that ... .* 1 Corinthians 10:1

> *... I would not have you ignorant.* 1 Corinthians 12:1

*For we would not, brethren, have you ignorant
of ... .*   2 Corinthians 1:8

*But I would not have you to be ignorant, breth-
ren, concerning ... .*   1 Thessalonians 4:13

It is not God's will for us to be always "in the
dark." He wants to speak to us, and He wants us to
hear His voice when He speaks. God doesn't want us
to be caught unaware by current events.

*But ye, brethren, are not in darkness, that that
day should overtake you as a thief. Ye are all the
children of light, and the children of the day: we
are not of the night, nor of darkness.*
                                    1 Thessalonians 5:4-5

God wants an informed people and has placed,
therefore, the gifts of the Spirit and the office of the
prophet in the Church for its edification and enlightenment. God wants us to know what is happening
before it is announced in the morning news.

Each New Years Eve we have a special service in
our church in which we all wait in the presence of the
Lord, expecting Him to speak to us and show us
what to expect in the coming year, so that we can be
prepared. Our members fast and pray in anticipation
of that service, and many share a word of prophecy
or a vision or revelation during the service.

One New Years Eve, God spoke to us very force-
fully. One of the unusual things that was said was

that there would come many days in which the stock market would swing wildly, more than 100 points one way or the other. This was fairly unusual at the time. A few days later a brother in California who had listened to the New Years Eve tape sent me a clipping from the Newspaper which told of the stock market dipping 101 points in one day.

One year, God told us that Iran and Iraq would end their hostilities toward the end of the year and would both turn their attention toward the Middle East. They did.

God wants an informed and prepared people. Didn't kings consult with prophets in days gone by, saying 'Is there any word from the Lord'? It will happen again, if we obey God and become informed in the Spirit.

Long before the savings and loan scandal, God spoke in the churches that many banks would fail. Long before the value of the dollar began to decline in world markets, God spoke about it to the churches. And He continues to prepare His people for whatever the future holds.

Prophecy Brings Wisdom

As we have seen, the Scriptures declare that the *spirit of prophecy is the testimony of Jesus* and that *the testimony of the Lord is sure, making wise the simple.* The spirit of prophecy makes simple people wise, and that's good enough for me. I want more of it.

You and I are *the simple*. There can be no doubt about that. But the Spirit of God will bring wisdom to each of us to cause us to be able to stand and make other *simple* men wise in God. We may not understand what God is doing, but we can declare it and watch God perform it.

None of us is wise enough to be able to give counsel to people concerning the very complex problems they are facing in modern society. If they talk to us about their problems, we don't know and understand all the circumstances involved and might give them the wrong counsel. But if God speaks to them through prophecy, what He says will be exactly what they need to hear.

We often limit our initial conversations with people who we may later be prophesying over. Then they are blessed when they see that God understands their problems and that the answers He gives are workable.

Many of us have experienced the need to hear from God about a certain situation and been in a place where we knew no one. But someone approached us and gave us the exact word we needed to hear. Nothing could be more critical for the difficult hour in which we are living.

Jesus said to His disciples:

> *I have yet many things to say unto you, but ye cannot bear them now. Howbeit when he, the Spirit of truth, is come, he will guide you into all truth: for he shall not speak of himself; but what-*

soever he shall hear, that shall he speak: and he will shew you things to come. He shall glorify me: for he shall receive of mine, and shall shew it unto you. All things that the Father hath are mine: therefore said I, that he shall take of mine, and shall shew it unto you. John 16:12-15

It is the work of the Spirit to guide us into all truth, to show us *things to come.* And, through the operation of the gift of prophecy, God makes known His ways to the simple and to the humble of heart.

Many people are hesitating with decisions because they are not sure of the will of God. They are asking themselves, "Should I?" or "What if I don't?" or "Maybe this isn't the time," and they need to hear specific instructions from God. Prophecy is God's tool of instruction. Each of us needs to know what God is requiring of us. And we can know that through the gift of prophecy.

Prophecy Inspires Faith

Prophecy inspires faith, taking things out of the future and bringing them into the present. Some say, "I know that someday my husband will get saved." But when a word of prophecy comes forth that now is God's time to save him, faith is generated, not for "someday" but for "now."

Many say, "I know that one day God will make it possible for me to visit the Holy Land." But when a prophetic word comes forth that they should prepare "now" to visit the land of God's people, their faith is taken out of "one day" and is focused instead on the present, and they begin to prepare to make the trip.

With the faith that prophecy inspires, we can better focus our prayers. When God has spoken to us about something He intends to do, it is easier to focus on that thing because we now recognize it as one of God's priorities. And focused prayers get answers.

Hearing directly from God stirs up great faith within us. When we do not have faith to reach out and appropriate from God, hearing from Him and knowing His will for us can stir up that faith and cause us to reach out and receive His answer.

Prophecy, therefore, brings understanding, enabling us to push aside doubts and fears and concentrate on God's express will for our lives.

Prophecy Acts As A Weapon Against Satan

You can fight against the power of Satan, using the prophetic word. Paul wrote to Timothy:

> *This charge I commit unto thee, son Timothy, according to the prophecies which went before on thee, that thou by them mightest war a good warfare;* 1 Timothy 1:18

We can hold the prophetic word up to God, expecting Him to keep His promises. And we can also hold the prophetic word up to Satan, knowing that God who has spoken will never fail and that His promise is a tool against Satan. Shake your prophetic promise in Satan's face when he comes to rob you, discourage you or cause you to doubt, saying 'God has spoken thus.' Use it to back him up and to get him off of your territory.

In 1968 I contracted Typhoid Fever in the Sudan. I was in Pakistan before I knew I had it, and if God hadn't intervened, I am sure I would have died in Asia.

Through days of extreme weakness, through high fevers and chills, I clung to one word of a prophecy my mother had given before I left home. The prophecy was spoken in July during Summer Camp, and by now it was October. But I remembered God saying, "Thou shalt go and return," and that was enough for me. Because of that simple word I knew that I would not die in some foreign land. I would *return*.

I clung to that promise through days and weeks of great trial. And I did return. I used that one word to back the devil up in a corner and to take back what belonged to me, my health, my strength, and my future ministry.

You can declare to the Enemy: "Thus saith the Lord God of Israel, 'Let My people go!' " And when he is reminded of the living word of the Lord, Satan must retreat. He simply has no recourse.

Prophecy Brings Unity

The prophecy of Ezekiel brought scattered bones together again, and the prophetic word brings unity.

God spoke to a brother from New Zealand in our campmeeting that he would be used to start a camp in his country, and that camp would be used to bring unity to the brethren there. Later, when I visited him, many of the ministers told me how grateful they were for the ministry of the camp he had established because it had brought unity among the believers.

Unity in the flesh is impossible. We all want it, but none of us can accomplish it. It is only the moving of the Spirit of God in our midst that can bring about the unity we all desire.

We need one another more than we ever have. As the Scriptures declare:

> *From whom the whole body fitly joined together and compacted by that which every joint supplieth, according to the effectual working in the measure of every part, maketh increase of the body unto the edifying of itself in love.*
> Ephesians 4:16

What one lacks should be made up by the abundance of another:

> *But by an equality, that now at this time your abundance may be a supply for their want, that their abundance also may be a supply for your want: that there may be equality:*
> 2 Corinthians 8:14

I need to draw from you, and you need to draw from me. It is only together that we can stand as a mighty army for God. The prophetic word brings about such a unity.

Prophecy Brings Excitement

We need some excitement in our churches today. It's no wonder we are losing our young people. We should have the most exciting show in town, but churches have become dull. It's no wonder we are losing so many husbands. Church has to compete with sports events and worldly entertainment. I can't blame many of those who have stopped attending certain churches. There is nothing there for them.

If we allow God to move as He desires to move, we can bring back our young people and our men that have been separated from the Church. The prophetic word of the Lord brings excitement into any service.

Back in the 40s, my parents had a small church in the city of Richmond that would seat about forty-five people. They had encountered a lot of opposition to their ministry and things were not going as well as they would have liked.

Then two brothers from out of town came and rented an auditorium in Richmond. It was in the early days of the revival later known as "latter rain," and the gifts of the Spirit, particularly prophecy, were being restored to the Body of Christ.

Those men of God laid hands on my father and began to prophesy. God showed my parents that He knew all that they had been going through and said, among other things, "A new day is yours. Enlargement is coming."

Things were so tight financially that my parents and our family were living from one meal to the next. But God said that He was about to raise them up and send them to the nations of the world and that they would preach to multiplied thousands of people.

Those were some of the strangest words my father could have heard at that time. They were so unusual, so unexpected, so out of reach of the natural mind. But, before long, every word that God had spoken began to come to pass. A noticeable change took place in our family and in the ministry of the church from the moment that prophetic word came forth and our family did indeed receive a worldwide ministry and my mother and father did preach to multiplied thousands of people.

This is why the devil fights prophecy. This is why the devil doesn't want you to prophesy to others. This is why he tries to keep you from yielding to God's move in your life.

Prophecy is exciting, and the devil doesn't want God's people to get excited. Nothing could be more exciting than hearing directly from the Lord!

I have found that people will stay up late at night and travel long distances when they are being ministered unto through the prophetic word. They get excited.

Prophecy Produces the Miraculous

When we prophesy in a great anointing, what happens is miraculous, just as miraculous as Ezekiel's dry bones coming to life. Anointed prophecy causes something to start stirring and to take on new life. And if those hearing the prophecy will respond, their lives will never be the same again.

I prophesied to a young pastor in Brisbane, Australia. He was a very capable person, but he felt that the church he had recently taken charge of was bigger than he could handle. In the prophecy God said to him that he would not only have success at home, but he would travel in ministry abroad, taking with him other members of the church.

Several years later, when he had already traveled several times in ministry to Singapore, to India, and to other places, he said to me, "Brother Heflin, at the time you gave that prophecy, those seemed to me like the craziest words I had ever heard. But our church is crowded, and we have been forced to purchase land on both sides of us to expand. Something happened to my soul when you spoke those prophetic words."

And it happens again and again. Prophecy produces the miraculous.

Prophecy Has Creative Powers

When Ezekiel prophesied in the valley of dry bones, those bones were lifeless. They were nothing but dead bones. But when the prophetic word was spoken, the dead bones became bones with sinews. Then they became bones with sinews and flesh. Then they became bones with sinews, flesh and skin. The prophetic word is creative and powerful. It can make things that are from things that are not.

We may not be able to see what is happening, but the word will be working until change comes, just as surely as God brought light out of darkness by His Word. There are no limits of time or space on God's word.

There was no sinew on the bones Ezekiel saw, but it was created by the prophetic word. There was no flesh on the bones when he first saw them, but after the prophetic word was spoken, it appeared. It was created by the prophetic word of God. There was no skin — until Ezekiel prophesied, and it was created. God has not stopped creating. He can do creative miracles for you too.

The word of the Lord has always possessed creative powers:

> *He sent his word, and healed them, and delivered them from their destructions.*
> Psalms 107:20

We will learn more about the creative power of prophecy as we go along.

Prophecy Enhances Ministries

In the nations where there has been little preaching of the Gospel, preaching in itself seems to be effective in reaching people for God. In our developed nations, however, people hear excellent preaching all the time. Any time of the day or night they can turn on the radio or television and hear some useful teaching from the Word of God. What they don't have, however, is personal revelation. And for that they need prophecy.

It is not eloquent speech that will bring you to world attention today, but God has promised:

> *A man's gift maketh room for him, and bringeth him before great men.* Proverbs 18:16

There are many great orators in the world today, some of them so well prepared in the Scriptures that they can dissect the Bible backwards and forwards. But there are not nearly as many who can hear from God and get a personal word for your life.

An *able minister* of the New Testament is not just a person who can preach. It is a person who knows how to *minister* God's blessings to others.

> *Who also hath made us able ministers of the new testament; not of the letter, but of the spirit: for the letter killeth, but the spirit giveth life.*
> 2 Corinthians 3:6

Too many have become ministers only of *the letter*. All they know is a theological argument. All they can present is a well-conceived homily. But what people need is God's power to change their lives.

Doors open to us when we can hear the voice of God and minister to His people through the gifts of the Spirit.

Preaching is fine, but people want to see something happen. Preaching without ministering to people is like preparing a meal for them and then not letting them partake of it. It's not right. It's not fair. People are hungry. Don't torment them by showing them the food and then not allowing them to partake of it.

When I hear someone preach a marvelous sermon, it gives me a desire to have them lay their hands on me and impart to me something in God. It causes me to desire to hear from them a personal word of prophecy over my life.

The same anointing that allows you to preach the Word of God can enable you to prophesy. The same anointing that allows you to counsel those who are hurt and confused will allow you to prophesy. You can tap into the resources of the Holy Ghost and be ready to prophesy in a moment's time. And this will bring revival.

If you can preach for an hour, but prophesy only fifteen minutes, you will have limited doors open to you. But if you can preach fifteen minutes and prophesy for an hour, there will be no lack of invitations.

When I was preaching in London some years ago, a group of ministers attended the meetings from an outlying area. They told me that they had been so discouraged with their ministries and with the fact that they never experienced any miracles from God that they had decided to set a time limit for action. If they didn't hear from God within a certain time and see Him working, they were going to quit the ministry and go back to their secular work.

We shared with them what God was doing all over the world. Then, before long, we laid hands on them and God began to show them their thoughts and their plans. And when they left that place they knew that God was still moving and working today and still speaking to His people.

Prophecy enhances any ministry.

Prophecy Paves the Way to A Bright Future

Many years ago, one of our sisters who was living in Jerusalem felt a great burden for the Canary Islands. She mentioned it in the daily prayer meeting that my sister has conducted for many years now in the Holy city, and they all prayed for the Canary Islands.

One week later news arrived in Jerusalem of the greatest aviation disaster in world history, and it happened that day in the Canary Islands. Two 747s, one belonging to KLM, Royal Dutch Airlines, and the other to Pan American Airways, collided on the runway, killing 542 and injuring some 70 others. Ten of the injured later died. Only about 60 survived the crash.

That evening, in the service, my sister, Ruth Heflin, stood and began to prophesy:

Out of the disaster, I will raise up a man with a worldwide ministry. He has not always been willing, but I will now answer the prayers of his mother and give him a ministry that shall bless the world.

The story of Norman Williams has now been told over and over around the world. Thirty years before the accident he had attended Pentecostal Bible School and, as a Spirit-filled young man, had ministered for a year. After this, however, he got involved in business and became very successful. He had never left God entirely, but his business interests took precedence and he had grown considerably cool in his spiritual life. His godly mother, however, continued to pray for him every day and to believe that one day he would obey the Lord and be in full-time ministry.

He sold his business to his partner and the partner decided to take a cruise with his wife before resuming control of the company. But when the time came to leave, the wife was too sick to go and Norman William decided to go on that cruise with his former partner.

When the two planes collided and burst into flames, those sitting beside Norman were killed almost instantly. The partner, who was sitting in front of Norman, was killed. But something protected Norman Williams from the intense flames. In the midst of the utter chaos of the crash, many promises of God came to his mind. One of them was:

When thou passest through the waters, I {will be} with thee; and through the rivers, they shall not overflow thee: when thou walkest through the fire, thou shalt not be burned; neither shall the flame kindle upon thee. Isaiah 43:2

Suddenly Norman William's eyes were drawn upward, and he saw a hole over his head. He was 52 and weighed 240 pounds so he could not propel himself through that hole, but somehow the Spirit of God lifted him up and got him through it. When he got out on the wing, he found that it was a great leap to the tarmac. It was, in fact, 35 feet. Others were jumping, and some were killed when someone else landed on top of them.

When his feet hit the ground, Norman Williams began speaking in tongues, something he had not done in a long while. He did not have a single burn, not even a singe. He had injured his ankle when he jumped from such a great height, but that was the only reminder he had of his ordeal.

He needed no other reminder. He knew that his life had been spared for a purpose and began preaching all over the world. His picture was on the front of Time Magazine and NewsWeek Magazine and newspapers around the world. His face appeared on television newscasts everywhere, and many doors began to open to him. He appeared on all the large Christian television programs. And his testimony was put into a book which sold in fourteen languages.

When he learned about the prophecy given in Jerusalem, he went there to visit Ruth and express his gratitude for the prayers of God's people. After the crash and his miraculous survival, he had resolved to give the rest of his life to the preaching of the gospel, but things had not gone well for him. When he heard that God had spoken in Jerusalem after the crash that out of the crash He would raise up a man with a worldwide ministry, his soul was set on fire afresh and he went forth to do the will of God.

When the story of Norman Williams was made into a film, the last portion of the film was done in St. Peter en Gallicantu, the church on Mount Zion, with my sister Ruth telling about the promise God had given there the day His life was snatched from the flames.

What He reveals to us can change the course of men's lives and head them toward a bright future.

Prophecy Brings About Change

In all of these cases, we have seen that prophecy brings about change. If you are afraid of change, don't become a prophet of God because prophecy brings change. If you don't want to shake things up everywhere you go, then don't become a prophet because prophecy brings change. If you don't want to be blamed for turning things upside down in a certain family or town or nation, then don't become a prophet of God because prophecy brings change.

Some people are satisfied and don't want their life to be disturbed. They are not candidates for prophecy because prophecy brings change. But, for those of us who are hungry for more of God, prophecy is a gift sent from Heaven. We are both ready to let God change us and to let Him use us to change the world around us.

- 3 -

Who Can Prophesy?

Who can prophesy is another of the raging contro-
versies about which there are many differing
viewpoints. Some believe that only a few designated
people, those recognized as "prophets," can prophesy. Others limit prophecy to the leadership of a
church. What does the Bible show us about who can
prophesy?

The Prophet Lives Within You

When you were filled with the Holy Ghost and
spoke in tongues, He came into you with all of His
potential, with all of His personality, with all of His
attributes, with all of His power, and with all of His
abilities. When you were baptized in the Spirit, therefore, you received the potential to manifest all nine
gifts of the Spirit, prophecy included. You don't have
to seek it; you already have it. You don't have to fast

and pray for it to come; it's already there. Just ask God to stir up what is already inside you.

The Holy Ghost lives in us. He dwells in our innermost being. And He longs to manifest Himself through us. Jesus said:

> *He that believeth on me, as the scripture hath said, out of his belly shall flow rivers of living water. (But this spake he of the Spirit, which they that believe on him should receive: for the Holy Ghost was not yet given; because that Jesus was not yet glorified.)*   John 7:38-39

God is in you. Let Him flow out of you to others. Prophecy is in you. Let it flow out to those who need to hear from God.

The Spirit of God has taken up His abode in our *innermost beings* and He is present to work miracles through us, to speak in tongues through us, to work special faith through us, or to prophesy through us. That is why St. Paul said to the Corinthians:

> *For ye may all prophesy ... .*
>   1 Corinthians 14:31

If prophecy were the domain of only a few, as many believe, Paul could never have made this statement. Prophecy is in you. *Ye may all prophesy.*

Just as the Spirit of God brings with Him His personality, which is then shed forth through us in the fruit of the Spirit, He also brings with Him His power, which, from that moment on, may be revealed through you in the gifts of the Spirit. The gifts of the Spirit are the manifestation of the presence of God in your life. He is the Healer. He is the Revealer of knowledge and wisdom. He is the Miracle Worker.

His presence in you makes you able to perform great things. Therefore, once He is within you, His entire potential is within you. You are not limited, therefore, to one gift or to several gifts. You may manifest any and all of the gifts of the Spirit — as the need arises and as you yield yourself to the Lord.

When Jesus stood on the last day of the great feast, He cried with a loud voice, inviting the people to come to Him to receive all that they lacked:

> *In the last day, that great day of the feast, Jesus stood and cried, saying, If any man thirst, let him come unto me, and drink.* John 7:37

That same cry goes forth today, but the difference is that now the river of His life is to flow out *through us*. Now His blessing goes forth *through us*. Now His word goes forth *through us*.

It's in there. Let the dams be burst, and let the rivers begin to flow. This is not something you must seek. You already have it.

When Paul was writing to Timothy, he declared to him:

> *Wherefore I put thee in remembrance that thou stir up the gift of God, which is in thee by the*

> *putting on of my hands. For God hath not given*
> *us the spirit of fear; but of power, and of love,*
> *and of a sound mind.*   2 Timothy 1:6-7

The gift had been in Timothy for some time already. It was dormant inside of him. He didn't have to ask for it. He just needed to stir it up, to allow it to manifest itself. He just needed to be obedient to the voice of the Spirit of God.

We don't receive the gifts of the Spirit on the installment plan. We don't acquire them little by little as we might a car or a house. We get them all at once, when we are filled with the Holy Ghost. They are there. Stir them up.

When I minister to groups of people to get them to move in the prophetic gift, I am not praying that they will receive a new gift. I am taking a great Holy Ghost spoon and stirring up the gifts lying dormant in them. That's all it takes, some stirring up. And when the gifts have been stirred up in you, you are ready to do exploits for God.

Many of the people God sends to our camp are sincere people that love the Lord and want to do His will. Many of them are already Spirit filled and the only thing they need is for someone to stir up the gifts that are within them. Many of them are stirred and prophesy for the first time while attending the campmeeting.

You can prophesy because we can *all* prophesy. The gift is in you. Stir it up. Allow the gift to operate.

In the Old Testament period, there was sometimes only one prophet alive at any one time. Now, in New Testament times, God has many people declaring His word. We don't have to import a prophet from another nation. God is raising them up in our midst. Every spirit-filled believer can taste of this privilege. So, you can prophesy.

The Vision of the Toolbox

In the early days of the Pentecostal outpouring in this country, there was a serious misconception concerning who could operate the gifts of the Spirit. Many early Pentecostal teachers took the phrase Paul used when speaking to the Corinthians: *"to one is given ..."* and decided that only one or perhaps as many as a few people in any one congregation could prophesy. They believed that each person had one predominant gift. If you were very spiritual, you might have two gifts. And if you were super-spiritual, you could conceivably have as many as three gifts, but no more.

My mother was raised in a church that taught this, and she grew up believing it. Dad, however, was a simple country boy, with limited formal education, and he brought to their lives and ministry a folksy wisdom. This teaching bothered him. He couldn't imagine that God gave you only part of Himself or that He would favor only a few in this regard, or that God's people were limited to one or two gifts. If the Spirit of God was in him, he reasoned, God could do whatever He wanted to through him, as the need of the hour required. Very early in his Christian experience, therefore, he came to the conclusion that every Spirit-baptized believer had all nine of the gifts of the Spirit.

This caused some friendly conflict between the two of them and, at one point, early in his ministry, Dad got serious with God in prayer about this matter and put before Him the questions: *Do we receive all of the gifts at once or do we receive them piecemeal, one at a time? Can only certain people operate certain gifts or can we each operate any or all of the gifts when they are needed?*

After he had been praying about this subject for a while, God gave him a vision of a carpenter's toolbox. He saw there a hammer, a square, a plumb line, a saw, a wood chisel, a screw driver, a plane and several other commonly used tools. When the carpenter goes to his work, God was saying to him, he picks up his toolbox and takes it with him.

He may not need everything he carries in the toolbox on today's job. He may only need a hammer and screwdriver today, but he can't be sure. So, he must take the whole toolbox because he doesn't know what job he will be called upon to do today. If he needs only a few tools, he has them on hand. If, however, he needs all the tools in his box, he will have no problem because they are all there available to him whenever he needs them.

That vision changed my father's life and ministry. He knew from that day on that it didn't matter what need arose, he had the tools he needed to deal with the situation. God had put all of heaven at his disposal. He need only call on the resources he required at any given moment.

I have often repeated his vision because it is the greatest revelation I have heard on this subject. If and when we need the tools of the Holy Ghost, they are at our disposal. It is that simple

If someone is demon possessed and you need discerning of spirits, it's there. If you need to lay hands on a sick person and bring them healing, the gifts of healing are in you — because God is in you. And if you need to prophesy, prophecy is waiting in your toolbox. Reach into the toolbox, take out the gift of prophecy and start using it for the glory of God.

If a need arises, and you have not become familiar with a certain tool, you may not be able to do a very good job with it. You will have to say, "I'm sorry. I've never tried to use this tool before. I wouldn't know how to hold it. I wouldn't know how to move it. I would be afraid of hurting myself or someone else. I can't do the job."

What a sad thing to have to say! So, familiarize yourself with the tools God has placed within you. They are present awaiting your orientation and use of them.

How can we think that God would send us to do a work without giving us all the tools that we need for the job? He wouldn't do that. All the gifts of the Spirit are available to us, as we need them, and as we are willing to use them. *Ye may all prophesy.*

We don't need to bring a talented person from a far place. We don't need to wait for the proper gift to come to us. God has already placed all the gifts and ministries in the Church.

Timothy was a young minister who needed a lot of advice from his spiritual father. Yet, when he was called upon to take a very heavy responsibility, Paul did not tell him that he would need to ask God for new gifts. He told him to stir up what was already in him. "I know they are there," he told him. "Just stir them up."

Each of us needs to stop waiting for something new to come to us and to move into the operation of the gifts that are already within us. The gifts of the Spirit are part of the power promised to believers by Jesus. He said:

> *But ye shall receive power, after that the Holy Ghost is come upon you: and ye shall be witnesses unto me both in Jerusalem, and in all Judaea, and in Samaria, and unto the uttermost part of the earth.*   Acts 1:8

The power of God works through the Holy Ghost that Jesus promised each of us. That power both gives us a desire to get out and let our lights shine toward others and gives us the ability to bring God's love to those who are in need of it. The power is in you because the Spirit of God is in you.

The prophetic ministry is for every spirit-filled person, and we must earnestly contend for it. If you are waiting for God to do something, let me tell you that He is waiting for you to start moving in the things He has already placed within you.

If you want to cook up a good meal, you go the cupboard or the refrigerator to get what you need. You take out some beans and some cabbage and some meat, and those of you who are good cooks know everything else that is necessary to put in the pot to make a nice dish. Well, God knows what we have need of and puts it all at our disposal. It is there when we need it because He is there when we need Him.

I don't have to pray for spirit-filled people that they receive the gift of prophecy. It is already in them because the Prophesier, the Holy Ghost, is already in them. All I need to do is stir up what they already have and encourage them to start using their gift for the glory of God.

A Matter of Controversy

My father's viewpoint became common knowledge among his peers, and other preachers would often gather around during campmeetings or ministers's conferences to rib him about this belief, which none of them shared. One day as he was approaching a group of preachers standing together, one of them said, "Oh, praise God, here comes that man who has all nine of the gifts of the Spirit at once."

"Well," my Dad replied, "let's test that idea. Have you ever prophesied?"

"Yes, I have," the man replied.

"Have you ever given a message in tongues?" my father asked.

"Yes, in fact, I have," the minister answered.

"And have you ever given the interpretation of a message in tongues?"

"Of course," was the reply to this question.

"Has God ever given you a word of knowledge concerning a given situation?"

"You know He has."

"Have you ever prayed for any sick person and they got well?"

And the answer, again, was affirmative.

In this way, one by one, my father made those ministers recognize that they did indeed have all nine of the gifts of the Spirit. They just hadn't recognized it. "You're the man with all nine of the gifts of the Spirit," he told them.

And if you will begin to examine what God has done in your life, you will quickly come to the same realization. The Spirit is there, so His power is there. The Spirit is there, so His abilities are there. He is the Prophet, and He is in you; so prophesy.

When my father first had this revelation, Mother told him not to tell anyone, as people would not receive it. One day he came excitedly to her after a morning teaching at the campmeeting in West Virginia and told her that Rev. Allen Swift, the morning Bible teacher, believed just as he did, that one person could manifest all nine gifts of the Spirit. From then on he spoke freely about his revelation.

Twenty Years of Seeking

In a minister's conference in Australia an elderly man came to me on the platform. He said, "Brother Heflin, please pray that I receive the gift of prophecy. I have been asking God for it for more than twenty years."

I shocked him when I replied, "I'm sorry, but I can't do that."

"I don't understand," he said. "What do you mean?"

I said, "I can't ask God to give you something you already have. It's already inside you. When He baptized you with the Holy Ghost, He placed in you the potential of all nine of the gifts of the Spirit. I will, however, pray for you that those gifts will be stirred up, that every fear will disappear, and that you will start using what you already have."

He said, "Well, I don't care how it happens. I just want it."

I laid my hands on him and began to rebuke every doubt and fear from his life. And, as I did, I could sense that something started moving down in his toes. I knew that God was doing something. When I had finished praying for him, I took his hand and placed it on my head, and that brother, who had waited twenty years for this moment, began to prophesy.

It was in him all the time. It just had to come out. He had spent twenty years asking God to give him a gift he already possessed. And this gift is resident in every spirit-filled believer. Start prophesying. Start obeying God. Speak out that which the Spirit puts upon your lips.

That man was scheduled to leave the same afternoon. His nephews had arranged to take him back home. But when he started exercising the gift of prophecy, he refused to go. He said, "Not me. I have found something I searched for over the past twenty years, and I am staying to get some more." And he did.

Don't waste your time praying for God to give you the gift of prophecy. You have it already. It's already inside you. It is the manifestation of the Spirit who has taken up residence in your innermost being. Let Him work — through you.

How I Learned This Truth

Don't feel badly if you didn't know this secret. I didn't always know it. In the early days of my ministry, I was preaching for a wise, elderly lady pastor in California. One day I was walking back and forth in her living room, pleading with God to use me and to manifest Himself through me in healing miracles. When she came into the living room and heard the way I was praying, she said to me, "Stop that!"

I was startled and asked what she meant. She said, "The anointing for healing the sick in within you.

Just get rid of all your fears about it, and it will flow forth through your hands and into the sick." And she was right.

I don't need to ask God to do it. He has already made provision for the *signs* that He said should *follow them that believe.* All I must do is get rid of my own fears and doubts, and God starts working. That power is within us.

Start prophesying. Open your mouth and let God fill it. Let God give you the words that men and women all around you desperately need to hear.

He is not in you in part. He is in you in full. He did not come into you with just part of His personality. He came into you with all that He is and all that He represents. As you grow in spiritual maturity, He can express Himself more and more through your life. But He is there all the time, all of Him.

If you have been baptized in the Holy Ghost with the evidence of speaking in other tongues, you can prophesy. It doesn't make any difference if you don't feel very well in the morning. God in you hasn't changed. You are still in a human body, and all human bodies are imperfect. But God has chosen to dwell in you, and nothing can change that.

When you wake up in the morning, you may not feel very powerful, especially before you have had your morning coffee, but that doesn't change the God in you. He is there — no matter how you are feeling at the moment. He is there — no matter how your personal life might be faring at the moment. He is there — no matter how your business may or may not be advancing at the moment. The God in you doesn't change.

I know that we experience highs and lows. At one moment we seem to be skipping and dancing over the tops of the waves of life's sea, and another moment we seem to be picking ourselves up off the bottom. But that doesn't change God in you. So you can't go by your feelings at the moment.

When I was younger in the Lord, I wanted to always see that the person I was praying for was feeling the power of God. I wanted to see them shake, and if they didn't shake, I wanted to shake them a little myself to be sure something was happening.

Then, I got typhoid fever and was so weak that I had to prop up my arm to even be able to lay hands on folks. But they still got healed anyway. This made me realize that it was not what I was feeling at the moment that counted, but what God was actually doing in the Spirit. Sometimes we feel it and sometimes we don't, but it doesn't matter if we do or not. If I believe God for the work to be done, He will do it — regardless of what I may be feeling at the moment.

During that period of sickness, I had no power within me to shake anyone. I could barely muster up enough strength to touch them on the head. But God did miracles for me in those days, miracles just as great as He had done at any other time. He is the Miracle Worker. We are only His conduits. We don't necessarily feel the same all the time. But it doesn't matter.

The word is in our mouths, and the anointing abides within us:

> *The word is nigh thee, even in thy mouth, and in thy heart: that is, the word of faith, which we preach;* Romans 10:8

> *But the anointing which ye have received of him abideth in you ... .* 1 John 2:27

Believe the fact that the gifts are within you, and stop spending time asking God for them. Believe that the anointing is within you, and stop spending time trying to work it up. Start looking for ways to use what God has already given you.

In a Catholic service in Australia, it was wonderful to see priests and nuns operating in the gifts of prophecy and word of knowledge. They had such a sweetness and innocence about them, almost like little children. It was refreshing to witness. Their advantage was that they didn't have a mountain of theology to overcome before they could get started. They just stepped out into the water and began walking. They were not speaking with earth-shattering force, but they were taking first steps, and it was beautiful.

This is the secret. Every person who has been baptized in the Spirit of God can do it, and God wants us to do it. We are, therefore, without excuse. If you have never prophesied, don't blame me. You can start today — if you want to. The same anointing that allows you to lay hands on the sick will allow you to prophesy. You can do it because the God of the Universe lives within you.

Each of us can have as many gifts as we will use for the glory of God and the upbuilding of His kingdom. *Ye may all prophesy.*

When you meet someone — on the street, in a public place, or wherever it might be — allow the gifts of the Spirit to operate through you to bring that person the blessing of God. God can place something in your spirit that will be the key to reaching them. And when you share with them what God has laid upon your heart, they will open as a flower and be amazed at how you know so much about them.

If kings were made to marvel when they received the witness of the prophets of old, men and women today should marvel at the power of God resident and manifested through you and me.

It is inside each of us. We don't need to order it COD. We don't need to ask for special delivery. We each have it.

Keep Your Battery Charged

If you used a car battery constantly and never charged it up, it would run down. That's the reason an automobile has an alternator. It keeps the battery charged. When you keep your battery charged, you can have confidence that when you need to use it, it will be available.

It is there. You may not see it. It is hidden under the hood of the car. But it's there, it's powerful, and it's waiting for you to turn the key.

The Holy Ghost is there. If you never call on Him, you will never see Him work. If you never have need of His power, you will not even be aware of His presence. Turn the key. Release that power. Take a step of faith. Move into action.

If God has placed His power in you, He wants it to flow out from you, to be manifested in you. He wants that power to work when you are on the job, when you are in the home, when you are in the supermarket, everywhere and all the time. The Holy Ghost lives in you seven days a week and twenty-four hours a day. Let Him work.

Many people have received the Holy Ghost baptism and spoken in tongues, but they have not gone any deeper in their experience. But that is just the beginning. The Holy Ghost power has a purpose, and that purpose is that you work the works of God. And you can. Prophesy in the Name of the Lord.

What Six Elements
Are Most Important
To Successful Prophecy?

I have noticed, in my own experience and in the lives of countless other ministers with which we have been involved through the years, that there are six basic elements to a successful prophetic ministry. If you learn these simple elements, God can use you and will use you for His glory.

Hearing The Voice of God

The first important element in a successful prophetic ministry is the ability to hear the voice of God.

The difference between a prophet and a priest in the Old Testament was that the priest stood before God representing the people, while the prophet stood before the people representing God. Therefore, a prophet had to maintain an intimate relationship with God and be capable of hearing what God was saying. And it is no different with the New Testament prophet. He or she must be capable of hearing from God.

If you have not developed the ability to hear the voice of God, you can never be a prophet or prophetess; for this is an absolute requirement. You cannot prophesy out of your own spirit. You cannot prophesy what you are hearing others say around you. You cannot prophesy the daily news or the latest novel. Prophecy must be from God. So you must be hearing from God.

Don't just be moved by excitement. Be moved by the voice of God. A prophet does not speak what he feels. A prophet does not speak what he thinks. We do not lay upon our beds before service time thinking up something that we intend to later speak forth in a service. Prophecy comes forth by the inspiration and the anointing of the Holy Ghost, and in no other way. So hearing the voice of God is the first necessary step.

The prophets of old were able to speak to others because they first heard the voice of God for themselves. In fact, much of what a prophet does is repeat what he hears God saying, as we shall see.

Obeying Without Question

The second important element in a successful prophetic ministry is an instant obedience to God.

When God called Jeremiah to be a prophet, he began to make excuses about why he could not do what God was calling him to do. We sometimes wonder why God doesn't use us more, but He is tired of all our excuses. It is time to lay aside every excuse and determine to obey God. Every prophet must learn complete obedience.

We are always thinking that maybe next year it will be more convenient for us to do what we couldn't seem do last year for the Lord. But we can go on making excuses forever, putting off till next year what we should be doing now. If we want to see God move, and we want to see His provision for our lives, the excuses must be laid aside, and we must start obeying the call of God upon our lives.

Jeremiah said:

I cannot speak.

That sounds like a pretty good reason to reject God's call. If you cannot speak, how can you be a prophet for God? But God didn't even dignify that excuse with an answer.

Next Jeremiah said, *"I am a child."* And this time God answered him, *"Don't say you are a child. I have sent you."* There simply are no acceptable excuses. It is time to lay aside all of our *I can't's* and to become God's mouthpiece.

If we insist on making excuses when someone calls on us, eventually that person won't call on us anymore. People will learn that we are unreliable and unresponsive. We may be planning to respond at some convenient moment, but we will probably never get the opportunity.

And if people get tired of our excuses, imagine how God feels! If we continue to give Him excuses as to why we cannot do things, He will be forced to raise up another person to take our place.

If you are guilty of offering excuses to God, let this be your day of change. Make up your mind today to stop offering excuses when God calls upon you to do something for Him. Learn obedience.

You may not seem to be as well qualified as others, but if God calls you, He knows what He is doing. You may not seem to be as well prepared as others, but God knows what He is doing. Stop worrying and start trusting God. If He has called you before you were formed in your mother's womb, He can take care of all the rest.

Your age doesn't matter. You are never too old to prophesy and never too young either.

Some fail to obey when they are sent to just one specific person, but that one person may be an Ethiopian Eunuch or a Cornelius or a Lydia. God knows what He is doing. Trust Him.

Some fail to obey because they are not sure what to say. But that is not your responsibility. God will put the words in your mouth.

If God calls you as a prophet to the nations, you may wonder where the money will come from for airline tickets and other travel expenses. When I was working as a salesman for a manufacturing firm (some forty years ago), they gave me a credit card that enabled me to travel on any airline. And I had a daily expense account. I wasn't expected to pay my own way. I was representing the company, so the company took care of me. Could God do any less for His people? If He sends you, He is obligated to provide your needs. Trust Him.

God will send you in the way that pleases Him. He isn't tied to one method or to one source. He has many ways of providing for you. Let Him use them all. Trust His goodness, and you won't have to live on a shoestring. You are worth a lot to God, so He will take care of you.

I once traveled for nine months with two wash-and-wear suits, but my faith has increased, and I know now that God can take good care of His children and let us travel in style, when we need to.

In those earlier days, I wasn't visiting presidents and ambassadors and dignitaries. But, although it takes more style to be well represented before those people, God is faithful to provide our every need. And the more valuable you become to God, the more He can trust you to speak His word, and the more He can know that you will put forth a suitable example for His Kingdom, the more He will send you to do His bidding.

Learn obedience. Do the work exactly as God wants it to be done. Reap the harvest exactly as He wants it to be reaped. Speak the word exactly as He wants it to be spoken. Be obedient to God. He said to Jeremiah:

Whatsoever I command thee thou shalt speak.
                                        Jeremiah 1:7

That is the role of the prophet.

Obedience is more important than ever in the days in which we are living; for, as God said to Jeremiah:

I will hasten my word to perform it.
                                        Jeremiah 1:12

If there was ever a time that we could say the Lord was hastening His word to perform it, it is the day in which we are living. God's clock is rapidly advancing, and He needs obedient people who will hear His voice and declare His will among the nations. You can help to hasten the fulfillment of the word of the Lord by obedience to God's plan for the end times.

By the time most of us get around to obeying God, the opportunity has passed and the anointing for that task has lifted, and we are left trying to figure out what happened. And the longer we postpone obedience in the gifts, the harder it becomes for us to act. Now is the day for obedience.

Repeating What You Hear God Say
or What You See In the Spirit

The third important element in a successful prophetic ministry is learning to repeat faithfully what you hear God saying or what you are seeing in the Spirit.

A brother from North Carolina accompanied me to Australia for ministry back in the late 70s. He had never prophesied over an individual before. One Wednesday night we had six hundred people come forward for prayer.

I said to him, "Brother, if you don't help me, we are going to be here all night. I can't do it all by myself. Get busy praying for people. Let God give you the words."

He started with a young lady. He closed his eyes tightly and prayed — as much for himself as for her. And as he prayed, he began to have a vision and began to prophesy according to what he was seeing in the vision. The young lady was broken and began weeping.

When he laid hands on the second person, he had a similar experience. God was showing him a vision for everyone he was praying for, and as he spoke forth what he was seeing in the vision, God was working on the hearts of the people. That was the beginning of a wonderful prophetic ministry that continued many years until God took him home.

This is the experience of many prophets who prophesy by vision. Others simply repeat what God is saying to them. That doesn't take any great talent. It simply takes a person who is hearing God and who will be obedient to speak forth what they are hearing or seeing God say.

This is the reason we don't need the entire prophecy before we begin. We just repeat the words as they come, and as we are speaking out the first part of the message, the Lord gives us the next part.

Standing in the Anointing

The fourth important element in a successful prophetic ministry is to learn to stand in the anointing.

When the Spirit nudges you to act, don't lose the opportunity. Step forward, raise your voice, and speak forth with an authoritative anointing so that everyone in the audience can hear what God is saying. Speak with enthusiasm. You are not talking about the weather or a new type of pizza that is available. You are speaking the words of God.

The prophetic word must come forth with great anointing. The measure of anointing you have will largely determine the measure of faith produced in the person who hears the prophecy. It you are not excited about what you are saying, how can you expect others to get excited about it? If you don't seem to believe what you are saying, how can you expect others to believe it?

When the opportunity to prophesy presents itself, you must be sure that the anointing you are under is greater than the anointing in which the service is flowing at the moment. If your anointing is less than the anointing in which the service is flowing, you will drag the entire service down, and your prophecy will not have the desired effect. It is best to keep silence in these moments.

It doesn't matter how profound the word God has given you to deliver, if it is not delivered in great anointing, it will not accomplish its purpose. Everything that is done in a service should lift that service a little higher. Otherwise, it will be a yo-yo meeting, with violent ups and downs of the anointing. And that is not productive. The anointing of the service should rise until everyone there is lifted into the very presence of God, and all things are possible. Therefore, let everything that is done be anointed and be uplifting. Learn the secret of pushing the anointing ever higher, and let everyone who participates learn the same secret.

As leaders, we must learn to put anointed people up to do things in the service, and as members we must work toward increasing the anointing of God upon our lives so that our part of the Body ministry may be effective. Let everything that we do add to the anointing.

Paul said to the Corinthians:

> *Even so ye, forasmuch as ye are zealous of spiritual gifts, seek that ye may excel to the edifying of the church.*   1 Corinthians 14:12

If your greatest desire is to be used of God, get a proper anointing upon your life and do everything for the edification of the entire Body. Learn what increases your anointing and do more of it. Learn what detracts from your anointing, and avoid it.

The longer you leave a tea kettle on the stove, the hotter it gets. Stay in the presence of God until your own soul is on fire, and you will be able to set others on fire too. Then prophesy in the anointing, and you will not be disappointed with the result.

Exercising Faith

The fifth important element in an effective prophetic ministry is the exercise of faith.

We make difficult something that God intended to be easy. Prophecy should be as easy as breathing. It is our fear that makes it so difficult. We are so intent on thinking through everything and analyzing it that we want to take out a slide rule and figure God out. Then we want to test it over and over before we are willing to step out in faith and obey God.

When you take a step of faith, contrary to the desires of your flesh, God will not disappoint you. He will be there to work on your behalf.

Prophecy, like the other gifts of the Spirit, works by faith.

The fear of failure is a strong force; so God said to Jeremiah:

Be not afraid.

And the reasoning behind His statement was this:

For I am with thee. Jeremiah 1:8

If God is with us, what do we have to fear? It is our flesh that fears. The spirit fears nothing. God is saying to each of us:

Be not afraid! Be not afraid! Be not afraid!

If you don't lose your fear of failure, you will never do anything for God.

The man who had only one talent was afraid that he would lose it, so he hid it in the ground. That act of fear caused him to lose everything. You cannot live in fear. You cannot walk in fear. You cannot act in fear. You cannot prophesy in fear. *Be not afraid.*

If we constantly hesitate to act for fear that we will be in the flesh, we stay in the flesh. Fear is not of God. It is the flesh that puts that fear upon us. But when we forget ourselves and our reputation and begin to take simple steps of faith, directed by the Spirit of God, the flesh has to take a back seat.

If God is in us, He won't allow us to make a mistake and fall on our faces. Let that confidence cause you to open yourself to the Spirit to be used of Him, as He wills.

If you expect to fail, you will fail. If you expect to make a mistake, you will make a mistake. If you expect to fall down, you will fall down. Fear will choke you and steal your victory.

God told us to be as little children. They are not born with fears. They have never failed and have no past to worry about, only a future.

Why are we afraid to fail when we are on the Lord's side? He has never failed. NEVER! He has never lost a battle. NEVER! It doesn't matter how difficult the task before us. If God is with us, we can do anything. ANYTHING!

If we could see the Lord physically present with us, it would relieve us of all fears. We need to begin to see Him in the Spirit and to know that He never leaves us, just as He has promised.

Be not afraid of the unknown. *Be not afraid* to take a risk. *Be not afraid* to step out by faith. *Be not afraid* of what other people may do or say.

Faith has two elements in prophecy. We must act in faith that we know God is speaking to us and that He will help us to deliver the message He desires, and we must believe that the word we have spoken will prosper and have a clear course to its fulfillment.

Believe!

Learning the Timing of God

The final important element in successful prophetic ministry is learning the timing of God.

There is a proper timing for prophecy, and that timing is extremely important. If you learn the proper timing, you can go anywhere in the world and be used of the Lord in this marvelous gift.

Improper timing is among the most common errors committed in the operation of the gift of prophecy. It is possible to jump in too early or too late, to jump ahead of the Spirit or to hold back until the best time for the prophecy has past. It is even possible, if the tone of the service has changed, to be completely out of order with a prophecy, giving it so late that it is intrusive rather than a blessing to everyone concerned.

There is a time for you to speak and there is a time for you to yield to others.

When I first got saved, we had few workers, and I was put to work right away. I had to lead the song service, take the prayer requests, receive the offering, and only then did I turn the service over to my father.

But on occasion, when I sat down, I felt something dropped into my spirit that was burning so that I felt I simply had to say it, but I didn't do it. If I had raised my hand, I know that my father would have given me the opportunity to speak. But the service was now in his hands, and I respected him enough to take my hands off of it and to let him run the service in his own way. So I prayed, "God, give my father the same thought." And before long he would say the very thing God had dropped into my heart — word for word. There is a proper timing for everything and a proper order for everything.

As a general rule, there are several times when it is always appropriate to prophesy in a church service. At the end of a prayer, when someone has gotten hold of God and prayed down the fire and the glory of the Lord, is an excellent time to speak out the message that is burning in your soul.

Another wonderful time for prophecy is at the close of a period of worship or at the close of a song. These are high moments of anointing when a prophecy will do the most good and be best received.

The person in charge of a service, usually the pastor or another member of the ministerial staff, sets the tone for the service. He or she must be sensitive to what God wants to do in that service and to guide it accordingly. This is the only way we can come together in unity. If that person has changed the order of the service and you insist on giving a prophecy that you have held back from giving earlier, you are out of order, and your words will, most likely, not bear the desired fruit.

The most important rule concerning timing, of course, is to get in the Spirit so that you will sense the timing of God, whether you are in a church meeting or anywhere else, for that matter. Know the timing of God.

Some people feel so anointed that they jump up and begin to prophesy before a song is finished or before a prayer is finished or before a time of praise dies down.

If you try to speak forth the message God is giving you while other activities are going on, or in the midst of the praises, while peoples' voices are raised, it will be difficult for others to hear you, and what you are doing will cause confusion.

But when you have a desire to do something for God, you will not make these mistakes. If you always prophesy because you desire to bless the church and never because you want to be exalted yourself, God will help you to know the proper timing to speak.

When you have learned the proper order for prophecy, and you prophesy within the framework of that order, it makes no difference whether the leadership of the church you are in or the membership of that church wants to recognize your message as from God. That is up to them. But if you have done it in order, the Lord will honor you — even if others do not want the word that God has given.

You may begin to give a word of prophecy at some point and someone else will jump up ahead of you and give more or less the same message. This should not be embarrassing to you but should show you that you had the mind of God. You will speak at another time.

If God gives you the same message that someone else has given, it is meaningless for you to repeat it, unless you have something to add to the first message. Rejoice that God has given you the message, but if someone else has given it first, remain in silence. Or, if there is opportunity, say to the people: "I can confirm the message given by ... because God gave me exactly the same message just before he/she spoke it out."

If you have a message, and the proper time passes, and the order of the service is changed, don't insist on giving your message later. Although all the other messages given flowed along with what God was giving you, because you delayed and did not give your message on time, it is now out of order. That doesn't mean that the message was not of God. It only means that it will not have the same impact if you give it now because you did not give it in a timely way.

The fact that your message flows in the same vein as others that are given proves that it is of God. But give it in the proper time. A message given out of time, drags down the anointing rather than lift it.

Anything out of time is limited in its effectiveness and may do more harm than good. There is a time for everything. And everything must be done in its proper time.

In the matter of timing, should you interrupt the preacher's message to bring a prophecy? Just be sure that the anointing you have is greater than that which is being exercised by the preacher. If it isn't, it is better to keep silent. Never do anything that will bring the anointing of the service down.

Some preachers feel that they are so important that they can never be interrupted. "I have prepared for many hours," they insist. "The Holy Ghost will not permit you to interrupt me while I am preaching." But the Spirit of God wants to control us all and if He wants to interrupt my preaching before I think I am finished and give the altar call, I welcome it. I am not too big for that.

I don't want carnal people to interrupt me, but I don't mind being interrupted by anointed people.

Get in the Spirit and learn the timing of God.

- 5 -

How Can You Get Started Prophesying?

Many people want to be used of God in prophecy, but they don't know how to get started. What do you do first? How can you get into this ministry? The answers to these questions are not difficult.

The Personal Preparation

Nothing can replace personal preparation. By this I don't mean that you have to memorize whole chapters of the Bible or spend years in a seminary classroom. But get yourself ready spiritually so that God can use you.

First of all, you must be filled with the Spirit to prophesy. This is one of the gifts *of* the Spirit and only operates through those who have been baptized in the Holy Ghost. The evidence that you have been baptized in the Holy Ghost is that you speak in tongues, so insist on waiting for this manifestation that will unlock many other treasures to you. Don't be influenced by those who say they received the Holy Ghost and spoke in tongues later. You will find that it was only after they spoke in tongues that power came to their lives.

Secondly, let God bathe you with His love. Chapter 13 of 1 Corinthians provides an essential element in the operation of the gifts of the Spirit and shows us that they operate according to the intensity of your love for others and your desire to bless them. If you have no desire to bless others, the gifts of the Spirit will not flow through your life. It is that simple.

The Holy Ghost doesn't pick you up out of your seat, open your mouth, and begin to move your tongue and form words. You have to get up; you have to open your mouth; and you have to form the words. And you will do it — if you love people and want to bless them.

It is the desire in you, the compassion of Christ working through you, that causes the manifestation of prophecy to come forth to meet the particular need of the people around you. The Scriptures declare:

> *But whoso hath this world's good, and seeth his brother have need, and shutteth up his bowels of compassion from him, how dwelleth the love of God in him?*   1 John 3:17

In the same way, if you know that you have power to deliver someone and set them free, and you do nothing, you will not be blameless before God. If you have the ability to hear the voice of God and relay His message to others and you do nothing, you cannot be excused.

Withhold not good from them to whom it is due, when it is in the power of thine hand to do it.
Proverbs 3:27

If each of us is charged with the power of the Holy Ghost and with the love of God, when we see someone in need, we will not wait for someone else to come along who might help them. If they are desperate enough, and we love them enough, we will say, "Let me lay my hands on you and God will deliver you." "Let me pray for you and see if God will give you the answer you need." If you don't love people in need, there will be no reason for God to work through you, for you will find no occasion for the operation of the gifts of the Spirit.

Furthermore, the personal preparation involves cleaning up your life so that you can be an example to others and so that you can generate respect in those to whom you minister. If people see sin in your life, or inconsistencies, or other indications of immaturity, they will have a hard time trusting the word that comes forth from your mouth, and you will lose your authority. You authority as a prophet for God is earned through a consistent Christian life-style.

All of us judge the value of prophecy by our impression of the person who gave it. We don't like to do it. We want to open to all of God's people, and we want to give opportunity to everyone. But if we know that someone is carnal and immature, we can't help but wonder how much of what they say can be trusted. Therefore, it behooves each of us to live a life that will cause our words to be respected.

Don't let your personal life cast doubt upon the things God wants to say through you. We have all heard the saying, "Actions speak louder than words." We must walk above reproach in the anointing, so that whatever comes out of our mouths will not be questioned.

Since hearing the voice of God is so important to the prophetic ministry, the personal preparation involves developing your personal relationship with the Lord to the point that you are hearing His voice on a daily basis and waiting in His presence until you are receiving revelation in other forms, as well.

Since obedience is such an important key, the personal preparation requires that you hone your sense of loyalty and obedience to God in the very smallest details of your personal life.

Since anointing is so important to successful prophetic ministry, anything that you can do on a regular basis to increase your anointing, such as fasting and prayer and living a life pleasing to God, will aid you immensely in your ministry of prophecy. You can't wait until you get to the church or some other place where you will prophesy before you get yourself ready. You have to be ready when the opportunity comes.

If you don't have a consistent prayer life, you will be dry and have nothing to give out. If you are to give out, you must continually take in. Therefore, a personal prayer life is essential in this ministry.

Fasting will cause you to grow rapidly, to leap frog over many others in the church and go on to greater things. Don't wait until the whole church fasts. Fast on your own. Make your own commitment to God.

And since faith is so essential to successful prophetic ministry, work to increase your faith. One of the ways you can do that is to exercise your faith in daily matters.

These are all part of the necessary personal preparation and represent, in a sense, the price that must be paid for the prophetic ministry. It is a very small price when compared to the vast rewards that await those who are obedient to the heavenly calling.

Elisha wanted a double portion of what he saw in the life of Elijah, but he had to pay a price before that double portion came upon him. It wasn't enough to go to Bethel. He had to go to Jericho. Jericho was where he had been living, and he had to make sure that things were right in his house. You can't expect to be a great prophet of God if you haven't set your own house in order. It is hypocritical to try to give advice and counsel to others when you haven't obeyed God yourself.

Get yourself straightened out. Get your own life in order. Get your own household in order. Let God's word take effect in your own life, and then you will be ready to speak His word to others. God wants to clean up your life so that you can help others clean up theirs.

If you are filled with bitterness and envy, how can you be sure that what comes from your mouth is not influenced by those very carnal feelings? If your spirit is wrong, the message will often be wrong.

One year a certain brother came to our campmeeting from Pakistan, a country that has been difficult for the Gospel because the majority of the people are Moslems, and Christians there face severe persecution. God told him that if he would be careful what went into his ears and what came out of his mouth, He would raise him up in a miracle ministry.

The brother fell on his face before God, recognizing that in every one of us, there are some things that are not pleasing to Him and asked God to forgive him. From that day forward he was careful not to listen to the usual gossip about fellow Christians and not to speak things that would be displeasing to God. And God kept his part of the bargain. That brother has had some of the largest miracle crusades in his country.

The Scriptures say:

> *Finally, brethren, whatsoever things are true, whatsoever things are honest, whatsoever things are just, whatsoever things are pure, whatsoever things are lovely, whatsoever things are of good report; if there be any virtue, and if there be any praise, think on these things.*   Philippians 4:8

If you are allowing people to fill your ears with trash about your fellow believers, how can you be sure that what is coming forth from your mouth is not influenced by the trash going into your ears? Begin to think pure thoughts and to avoid impure words.

Get yourself ready to be used of God. Develop a life of meditation on the things of God. Paul wrote to Timothy:

> *Meditate upon these things; give thyself wholly to them; that thy profiting may appear to all.*
> 1 Timothy 4:15

Most of us don't relate this particular verse to the gifts of the Spirit. What are we to meditate upon? What are we to give ourselves wholly unto? What will cause our profiting to appear to all? All of these statements follow directly the phrase *"Neglect not the gift"* in verse 14.

We are to meditate upon the things God has entrusted to us. We are to give ourselves wholly to them. If we do, our profiting will appear to all. These are wonderful promises. And they are followed by another great promise:

> *Take heed unto thyself, and unto the doctrine; continue in them: for in doing this thou shalt both save thyself, and them that hear thee.*
> 1 Timothy 4:16

Living a life of holy meditation will result both in personal salvation and the salvation of many others, *them that hear thee.* What a great promise!

Since the gifts and manifestations of the Spirit are just that, of the Spirit, it behooves us all to learn to live and walk in the Spirit. God has commanded us to *be filled with the Spirit:*

> *And be not drunk with wine, wherein is excess; but be filled with the Spirit;*   Ephesians 5:18

He has commanded us to walk in the Spirit:

> *This I say then, Walk in the Spirit, and ye shall not fulfil the lust of the flesh.*   Galatians 5:16

We are to be a people *led by the Spirit of God:*

> *For as many as are led by the Spirit of God, they are the sons of God.*   Romans 8:14

This filling of the Spirit, walking in the Spirit, and being guided by the Spirit was not meant to be a periodic thing, a hit and miss thing, or an occasional thing. God wants to fill us daily, to cause us to walk with Him always and to guide us hourly.

The Importance of
A Good Example To Emulate

When Elisha asked Elijah for the double portion ministry, Elijah responded, *"You have asked a hard thing."* But Elisha wasn't concerned about how hard it was. He wanted it, desperately and was willing to pay whatever price was necessary. He refused to leave the prophet's side.

This is another important key to entering into the prophetic ministry. If you want to become a prophet, find a great prophet and stay close by his or her side, learning all you can, receiving all you can from them through impartation.

Elisha sensed that if God had done it for Elijah, He could do it for him also. He was absolutely right. No one holds a copyright on God's gifts. No one has an exclusive right to God's great power. What He has done for another, He will do for you.

Elisha was smart enough not to think that he could simply imitate what he had seen in the life of his mentor. He was smart enough to sense that he needed to open himself up to God and receive something special for himself. He saw that Elijah's greatness was because of the touch of God upon his life and was convinced that if he got a similar touch from God, or an even greater touch from God, upon his own life, he could do the same miracles Elijah had done and even greater miracles. And he did.

It worked for Joshua when he stayed close to Moses long enough, and it has worked for countless others. This is an important secret. By staying close to someone who is used of God you can not only learn from them how to have the anointing they have attained, you can move beyond it.

When Elijah's mantle fell from him, Elisha ran and grabbed it. Then, almost immediately, he put to the test what he had learned. He had watched as Elijah smote the banks of the river and had seen the miracle of the parting of the waters. Now, he boldly took hold of that same mantle and smote the waters, crying out, *"Where is the Lord God of Elijah?"* And when he did, the waters parted as they had for Elijah, because God is no respecter of persons.

If you do find some great man or woman to emulate, be careful. In the end, your strength and insight does not depend on another prophet. It comes from God. When that person is dead and gone, or when that person is taken away to another country, or when that person moves on to another city, or (God forbid) if and when that person loses, for some reason, the touch of God upon their lives, what you are and what you do does not depend on another prophet. If God has called you, then your ministry will stand or fall on its own — regardless of what others do.

The Necessity of Humility

Nothing could be more important in the prophetic ministry than learning humility. If God foresees that by allowing you to be used in this gift, you will become exalted and your spiritual life will be harmed, He is obligated not to raise you up. His love compels Him.

As always, the way to go up is to go down. James wrote to the churches:

> *Humble yourselves in the sight of the Lord, and he shall lift you up.* James 4:10

Peter wrote to the churches:

> *Humble yourselves therefore under the mighty hand of God, that he may exalt you in due time:* 1 Peter 5:6

Jesus Himself said to His disciples:

> *The scribes and the Pharisees sit in Moses' seat: All therefore whatsoever they bid you observe, that observe and do; but do not ye after their works: for they say, and do not. For they bind heavy burdens and grievous to be borne, and lay them on men's shoulders; but they themselves will not move them with one of their fingers.*
>
> *But all their works they do for to be seen of men: they make broad their phylacteries, and enlarge the borders of their garments, And love the uppermost rooms at feasts, and the chief seats in the synagogues, And greetings in the markets, and to be called of men, Rabbi, Rabbi.*
>
> *But be not ye called Rabbi: for one is your Master, even Christ; and all ye are brethren. And call no man your father upon the earth: for one is your Father, which is in heaven. Neither be ye called masters: for one is your Master, even Christ. But he that is greatest among you shall be your servant. And whosoever shall exalt himself shall be abased; and he that shall humble himself shall be exalted.* Matthew 23:2-12

If you can learn to humble yourself before God, you can then stand strong and tall before man, representing the Lord of Glory in all of His authority. When self is crucified and set aside, it is then that God can do something with your life, but not until.

When God begins to use you, you must guard constantly against pride — a most insidious evil. God is a jealous God and will not share His glory with another. When pride begins to come in, His anointing will begin to depart.

None of us is immune to the temptation toward pride. I have been in services where everyone seemed to get healed and in the midst of all that glory of the manifested power of God, I would have the devil himself say to me, "My, aren't you anointed tonight!"

I had to say, "Satan, you get out of here right now." And then I had to ask God to forgive me for even a moment's thought that I deserved what He was doing for me or was, in any way, better than someone else because of His touch upon my life. I cannot afford pride. It is a killer.

> *When pride cometh, then cometh shame: but with the lowly is wisdom.*   Proverbs 11:2

> *Only by pride cometh contention: but with the well advised is wisdom.*   Proverbs 13:10

> *Pride goeth before destruction, and an haughty spirit before a fall.*   Proverbs 16:18

If the Devil can succeed in any way in causing you to take the glory for yourself, he has won a great victory, and you will notice the glory diminishing in your life and ministry. God will leave you standing alone before the people, and He will do it because He loves you and cannot stand by while you are destroyed by pride. When He sees pride creeping in, He must immediately turn back the dial of His glory — to preserve your soul.

All glory belongs to God, and when you are faithful to lift Him up and Him only, He will continue to send miracles your way and will continue to give you His word for others.

The more God uses you, the more humble you must become. Don't fall into the trap of pride. Great men and women are humble. Don't ever forget that fact.

> But he giveth more grace. Wherefore he saith, God resisteth the proud, but giveth grace unto the humble.   James 4:6

Let God do the exalting. He will do it *in due time.*

The Proper Atmosphere

When you have a desire to get started in the ministry of prophecy, it is helpful to find a proper atmosphere. Many churches are not willing to give opportunity to the uninitiated, so they remain uninitiated. How can we learn if we don't have an opportunity?

Sometimes it is not the leaders who are to blame. Many people hold back in the gifts because they recognize that they need perfecting. And these are not bad people. Many of them start out in great zeal exercising the gifts. Then, when they begin to realize that they are not perfect, they draw back. This would seem to be a wise thing. But how can God perfect us if we are not moving in these gifts? How can we learn if we don't try?

Get into an atmosphere where the gifts of the Spirit are flowing, where you will not be constantly worried about what someone might do or say, and where everyone is given an opportunity to operate the gifts. Get into an atmosphere where you can open yourself up to God without reservation.

If you have a past, it is better for you to go somewhere where you are not known. That way you won't be worried that everyone is thinking about your past and rejecting what God is saying through you. It is easier to begin prophesying in a place where nobody knows you. That way the Devil cannot put such fears into your heart and mind.

If, however, you cannot go somewhere where you are unknown, begin anyway. If you cannot escape your past because it is too widely known, begin anyway. Don't let what people think keep you from obeying God and beginning to exercise the gifts that the Spirit of God has deposited in your life. Take advantage of every opportunity and don't hold back.

Get around the altar area praying with those who are hungry for God. Then believe for the moment when you can stop praying and start speaking out the word God gives you.

The Required Action

If God is urging you to prophesy, He knows where you are . He knows who is present. Obey Him. Stand up, open your mouth and speak forth.

There must come a moment when you make a claim on what God has promised you, and you begin. You will never get very far if you never get started. Don't wait for some sign. Don't wait for someone else's urgings. Don't wait until someone has to rebuke you for your slowness in obeying the voice of God. Begin.

Stop delaying. Just believe God and begin.

God will not ask you to do something that you cannot do. He will not ask you to do something that will only lead to personal embarrassment. He will not lead you to do something that will not be beneficial for the entire Body. Just hear His voice and obey.

All of us are still living in human bodies. We are all flesh and blood. And, because of that, there is always the opportunity for Satan to inject an element of fear into our hearts concerning prophecy, particularly if we are just beginning.

Once you have prophesied a few times and seen God bring to pass what you are speaking, you lose the fear and are encouraged. It is like swimming. Sometimes you just have to get out in the water and start doing it. As long as you remain on the shore, the fear of drowning will always be present. When you have been in the water before, however, you have no fear of jumping right in.

You might have some concern about swimming in new waters. If that is the case, you just get out into the water and explore it a little so that you can become accustomed to your new surroundings. When you see that you can swim in the new place as you were able to do in other places, you realize that it's just swimming, and that you can do just as well, anywhere you happen to be at the moment. If you can do it in one circumstance, you can do it in another. And God is calling us all to swim in new waters, to run in new places.

Take off your comfortable shoes and put on some running shoes instead. If you have just been plodding along for God, get serious about His work and start moving with determination. Step up the pace. Get the feel of what God is doing in this hour. He is hastening His word.

Lay aside anything that seems to be weighing you down:

> *Wherefore seeing we also are compassed about with so great a cloud of witnesses, let us lay aside every weight, and the sin which doth so easily beset us, and let us run with patience the race that is set before us,* Hebrews 12:1

Get rid of every hindrance and start running.

God has ordained us; He has put His words in our mouths; He has prepared us for service; and He is hastening us forth. Take the required action.

The Necessary Precaution

When you open your mouth and say, "Thus saith the Lord...," let the words that come forth always be what the Lord is saying. People don't need your opinions. They won't be blessed by your feelings. Give them a word from God.

If you tell me that you have an idea, I may or may not have time to think much about what you are saying. But if you tell me that you have heard from God, I am going to take time to listen carefully to what you are saying. It makes all the difference in the world. So be sure that you are hearing clearly what God is saying.

The details that God gives you to speak forth in prophecy are important because they will cause the person receiving the message to realize that what you are saying is from God and to listen carefully to the rest of the message. Believe God for detail. This is what distinguishes prophecy from talk. Talk is cheap. It is sometimes helpful, but often not.

Let the words you speak be inspired. God doesn't make mistakes. You cannot play with the gift of prophecy. You cannot say to someone later, when their life has been shipwrecked, "Sorry, we all make mistakes." You can't make a mistake when you are saying, "Thus saith the Lord ... ."

Nobody will have confidence in a prophecy that they believe may be half right and half wrong. Nobody will feel wise enough to sort out the bad 5% of a prophecy that is 95% right. This is too important to play around with. Get it right the first time.

That is not to say that you have to be perfect to begin. But while we may not be perfect, we can live in the realm of fasting and prayer until God gives us His thoughts. And then we can speak with assurance that what we say is from Him. Before you minister, ask the Spirit of God to cover your mind with the blood of Jesus and to prevent you from speaking a word that would not be pleasing to God.

If you live a life of halfheartedness, you may be in danger of saying the wrong things. But if you live in the fear of God, when you open your mouth, God will help you to speak what needs to be heard.

There are severe warnings in Scripture to those who would dare speak their own mind and try to say it is the word of the Lord.

> *But the prophet, which shall presume to speak a word in my name, which I have not commanded him to speak, or that shall speak in the name of other gods, even that prophet shall die.*
> Deuteronomy 18:20

Don't presume anything. Fast and pray and stay in a place of close communion with God. Keep your flesh under subjection to the Spirit of the Lord and you will speak what God desires and not what you desire yourself.

My Own Experience In Getting Started

I didn't always exercise this gift. Although I had seen my mother prophesy over people for years, somehow I hadn't appropriated it for myself.

Then, in 1969, I was in Ajmir, India and an Indian brother was being ordained to the ministry. I felt that God wanted to speak to him and there was no one else there who could do it, so I felt forced to do it. When I had finished prophesying over him, several other ministers jumped up on the platform and indicated that they wanted to hear from God too.

That really stretched my faith. Prophesying over one person was one thing, but prophesying over several others was something else entirely. I had to call on the resources of heaven to help me. And before I had finished I had prophesied over six or seven ministers.

The following year God sent me to Australia. I preached in a church where the pastor was away and a visiting minister was in charge. I thought we had agreed together in advance how the service would run, but to my surprise the man changed everything. He said to the people, "Brother Heflin has been a blessing to us. Let us come forward and bless him." And, with that, they laid hands on me and many of them had a word from heaven for my soul. It was marvelous.

Then he asked me, "Are you ready?"

I wasn't sure what I was ready for, but I said I was.

Then he said, "Everyone who wants Brother Heflin to lay hands on you and pray for you, get in a line and he will minister to you."

That line seemed to me to be several blocks long. I had never seen such a throng of people. "Oh, God, help me," I prayed as I laid my hands on the first one. After that first glance, I was afraid to look at the line. It was all I could do to face the people one at a time.

My, was I stretched that day, but, I thank God for the experience. It did me a world of good, and I have never looked back and have made prophecy an integral part of our ministry all over the world.

I promise you that if you make up your mind to be used of God in this way, nothing will be able to hinder you.

Getting started is the most difficult thing for most people. There has to be a starting point. This is the reason we make it so easy for people to prophesy in our meetings. We often call everyone to the front, tell them to lay hands on each other and believe God for a word for each other.

You have to start somewhere. And, as we have said, when you have gotten over those initial fears, the gift begins to flow in your life. Here are some practical teachings that will help you get started in the ministry of prophecy.

When To Prophesy?

How do you know when God is moving upon you to give a prophecy? Sometimes several words, or a thought or a vision come to you, and you sense that it is not just for you personally but for the entire group. At others times, the Lord will impress upon you the need to prophesy without giving you any prior words or thoughts or vision. And when He does, you just open your mouth by faith and begin to speak, and it comes. Make yourself available to God and He will put the words in your mouth.

You don't need the message in advance. The Lord is in you and the message is from Him. Let Him speak. It would be easy to prophesy, and anyone could do it, if God gave you the entire prophecy at once.

That would not require faith. But when you have only a few words or a single thought, you must act in faith upon what God has already given you and He will give you more — as you speak out what you already know.

Usually all that we have is a starting point, nothing more. When you are ministering to individuals, you may receive just a word. That word might be "doubt," "unbelief," or "fear." At other times you may have an insight concerning guidance or direction, and that is all you have. So you start with what you have, and as you do, God will continue to give you thoughts until the prophecy is complete.

Sometimes you will begin to see a vision. Some visions are just for you and are not to be shared with others. But when you have a vision that is for the benefit of another or for the whole congregation, you will also receive a sense that this vision is to be shared. As you begin to speak forth what you are seeing, that is the beginning of your prophecy. Continue to speak it forth until the vision fades or until God gives you other thoughts or words to express.

Prophecy does not have to be long. It might simply be "Let My people go." The quantity of words is not important, but the clarity of the message is important. It can be done in very simple words and phrases. Just speak them out and watch as God works for you.

When To Stop Prophesying?

One of the problems that confronts those who are new to prophecy is not when to prophesy but when to stop prophesying. Some people go on and on, repeating or embellishing what they have seen or felt or heard or perceived, until all anointing is gone from it. They are almost like an old fashioned alarm clock that keeps ringing until it runs down. Stop while the anointing is still heavy upon you. Just because you still feel the anointing of the Spirit of God doesn't mean you must keep on talking until you run down. Learning when to stop is just as important as learning when to start.

When you sense that you have delivered the word God has placed on your heart, when you have expressed the thought God has given you, when you have described the vision God has shown you, stop. There are always many more details that you could add, but if you insist on doing it, you will spoil the impact of what has already been said and bring confusion.

Making a prophecy longer does not necessarily make it better, and a person can only remember so much. Each of us is limited in that respect. That is why the Lord usually doesn't speak to us for hours on end and tell us absolutely everything. He gives His revelation to us: *line upon line, precept upon precept, here a little and there a little.*

Say what God wants to say, then stop. Don't insist on dragging the messages out. A short, anointed message is better than a long, halfhearted one.

During the years I was in sales, I would sometimes realize that I had said too much, that I had made a mistake and should have stopped while I was ahead. Usually it was already too late to correct the mistake, and I lost the sale. Know when to stop.

Ignore People's Appearance

When you are praying for an individual, you stand there and look at that individual, and you are wondering what God might want to say to him or to her. You could stand there all day looking at the person and not come up with anything at all because appearances are so deceiving. Forget appearances.

When I was preaching in Australia, the pastor invited one of his colleagues who desperately needed an answer from God. He told him to come dressed as others and that he would purposely not tell me that any other preachers were present. Three men came forward for special prayer that night. One of them was a successful farmer; the second was a young man who had been promoted in the court system of Australia; and the third was the preacher. If they had told me beforehand that the three had such diverse responsibilities and asked me to pick out which was which, I could not have done it. They all looked alike to me.

But God knows who we are, and He gave a word to the farmer that related to his farming; He gave a word to the attorney relating to his court duties; and He gave a word to the preacher concerning his ministerial responsibilities.

You simply cannot look at how a person is dressed and know much about them or know what God wants to say to them. You must look beyond the appearance. Ignore it.

When Isaac had grown older and his eyesight was dim, he laid hands on Jacob, thinking that it was Esau, and prophesied. But God knew exactly who was receiving the blessing of his father, and the word that came forth was consistent with the promise of God to Jacob. God never makes mistakes. He knows the hearts of men.

Jacob deceived Isaac by putting on the clothes of his brother and by covering his arms with animal skins. But God was not fooled. He knows the hearts of men.

When I stand before a person that I know needs a word from the Lord, I am praying, "God, You know that I don't know this person. You know that I don't know their name or anything about them. I have no clue as to what to say." And, as I pray, I am waiting for the Lord to reveal to me how to begin. When I get a word or a thought or a vision, I can begin to prophesy. Until then, I must wait in His presence, worshiping Him in the Spirit; for He is the Prophesier. I am just *the voice*.

I ignore the appearance and depend entirely on the Spirit of God to reveal the thoughts of men's hearts.

And don't keep looking at their faces. The face may not tell you much. Close your eyes, if you have to, to look beyond the face and the rest of the physical appearance and look into the soul — through the Spirit of God.

Open Your Mouth and Begin

You cannot prophesy with your mouth shut. In the same way that you cannot receive the Holy Ghost baptism with speaking in tongues if your mouth is closed and you are silent, you must open your mouth and begin talking in order to prophesy.

Never be afraid to say, "Thus saith the Lord ... ." Your boldness in beginning brings forth a greater anointing upon you. Sometimes you actually feel led to say those introductory words before any revelation has come, and your revelation will come as you are saying the introductory words. That may be scary at first, but when you have experienced it many times, you know what God can do, so you lose your fear.

In a sense, speaking those first words is much like priming an old-fashioned pump. The introductory words gets the flow of prophetic revelation started.

Begin!

Don't worry about what you will say next. If God gave you the time to write down the prophecy and to edit out the bad grammar and make it sound better before you gave it, you would probably take out the most important parts, parts that you didn't understand or appreciate as being important but which the listener will understand immediately.

Prophecy is miraculous and spontaneous. Just obey.

Some people have visions of prophesying to the nations but they have not been obedient to God in the local setting. God will never use you as a prophet to nations until you have first taken a step of faith in prophesying locally. Every level of prophecy demands a greater anointing, and a greater life of revelation and insight.

Get started where you are. When you feel the anointing to prophesy, don't wait for others. Open your mouth and obey God.

Speaking begins to put you in "control" of the situation, in a business manner of speaking. To gain further control, let God give you the key to that particular situation. There is a key to every situation and God will show you just what to say to take control of the situation and to guarantee victory.

Give Prophecy A Prominent Place In Ministry

Sometimes every word that we pray over a person could have been prophesied. Indeed, our prayers are often prophetic. While we are praying, we feel led to say, "Lord, You know about that situation at home. Take care of that." We didn't know anything about what we were led to call a "situation at home," but God did, and He revealed it to us. And, on the basis of His revelation, we spoke that phrase forth in prayer.

Some people will recognize that we are speaking by revelation, but others will not. In their case, therefore, we need to say what God is showing us in the most forceful way, which happens to be: "Thus saith the Lord ... ."

When I was young in the ministry, I noticed that when I began to pray for people, God was showing me things about them. As I called out in prayer the things God showed me, I noticed an emotional impact upon the person I was praying for. They would be responding, "Yes, Lord," because I was getting down into the area that was bothering them the most.

Later, I realized that I could use that same insight into the situation to begin to prophesy and to make a greater impact on people's lives, and I have done it ever since.

I have found that when you speak forth some of those hidden things, you catch the attention of the person and he or she knows that what you are saying is from God. Then the Lord can say some other things He wants to say to that person, and they will listen because of the impact your first words have made on them. I find this much more effective than a simple prayer over a person.

The act of saying, "Thus saith the Lord" changes everything.

A prophetic word is far more effective than a time of counseling in which we simply discuss the problem at hand. In fact, much of the "counsel" that is going on today is fleshly counsel and needs to be replaced with "thus saith the Lord."

A word from the Lord can do much more for someone than my sharing with them my experience. A word from the Lord can do much more for someone than my understanding or my commiseration. My commiseration may have some limited psychological impact, but the word of God will change a man's life — eternally.

If you are willing to give prophecy a more prominent place in your ministry, the revelations you receive while you are praying can be handled in a more forceful way. You might say: "Thus saith the Lord. Fear not, and do not be concerned; for I will take care of that situation at home." In many circumstances, this would be the most powerful and productive way to present the truth God has given to you concerning His desire to take care of that "situation at home."

God will show you other ways that you can give prophecy a more prominent place in your ministry.

Trust What God Is Showing You

Satan is always telling us to be careful, that what comes out of our mouths might not be of God, and we sometimes listen to him because we are concerned about protecting our reputations.

I was praying for the members of a congregation in Australia for the first time. During the day, I had been praying that God would increase my ability in the word of knowledge. When I started praying for one man, I asked him what was wrong. "I need you to pray for my eyes," he said.

I started praying, "Oh God, heal this brother's eyes ... " and I found myself starting to say, "so that he can read those blueprints without difficulty." But I wondered where that thought came from and, to protect myself, said, "so that when he reads that fine print, he will have no difficulty."

When I had finished praying, I asked him, "What kind of work do you do?"

And he answered, "I'm an architect."

I was ashamed then that I had not been willing to speak out what God had shown me. God had put the words in my mouth, but I wasn't bold enough to declare them. Fear had robbed me.

But what do we have to fear? If God gives us the words, He knows why we are saying them, and usually the person we speak them to will understand what is being said — whether we do or not.

When you ask God to give you something, believe what He is giving you. If you are having an unusual thought, there must be a reason for it. I had no reason to believe that the man read blueprints. Why did that thought come to my mind? I hadn't been thinking about architects or blueprints. If we have no ulterior

motives in thinking a certain way, we can trust that
what we are sensing is from God.

If we take a step forward and use what God is
giving to us, He will give us other "inside information." And if we fail to use what He is giving, we will
actually begin to slip backward in our spiritual per-
ception.

Trust God. He knows what He is doing.

Proceed With Seriousness

Some people have asked how to get others to take
prophecy seriously. Well, the most important thing
is to let them know that it is coming from God and
not from you. You might begin by saying:

> *"Behold, I say unto you ... ."*
> *"The Lord would say unto you ... ."*
> *"Thus saith the Lord ... ."*

Or any such similar statement.

If you just speak in a normal conversational tone
and use normal conversational phrases, people will
not take your message seriously.

Some people have decided to do the opposite.
Rather than risk saying, "Thus saith the Lord ...,"
they have decided to speak their revelations in safe
ways: "Brother," they say, "I have a feeling that ... ."
Their attempt to play it safe removes all the power
from what they are saying. I am not really impressed,
for the most part, with what someone "feels" or "be-

lieves" or "thinks" or even "senses." That's too dangerous. I want to know what God is saying.

Much of what we speak in conversation is guided by the Spirit or God, but because not all parts of our conversation are guided by the Spirit, people find it hard to accept some advice that we may be positive came from God. If we are positive that it came from God then we need to say it came from God and speak it forth with seriousness.

Many of us get a word of knowledge while we are talking to people. But unless we can include that word of knowledge in a prophecy, it will often not have the desired impact.

There is something about hearing directly from God that is thrilling. When those anointed words are spoken, "Thus saith the Lord ... ," a thrill splits the air and people actually gasp with anticipation.

Proceed with seriousness when you prophesy.

Don't Worry About Understanding

Say exactly what God tells you to say and stand by it — whether you understand it or not. If you know that it was from the Lord, don't worry about anything else.

Sometimes even the person receiving the prophecy will not understand the words we speak. Then, a few days later, something will happen to them, and they will suddenly understand completely what it was all about.

You may, at some point, understand what you have spoken. But that is not the important thing. You are just *the voice*. Don't worry about understanding. You are just a conduit. You don't have to understand it. You just have to speak it forth.

If you can receive understanding, it's better because you may be able to help the person receiving the prophecy to understand. Just as God gave the ability to understand dreams and visions and hard sayings to His prophets of old, He may use you to bring understanding to the people around you. But if not, that's okay too.

There may be a very good reason that you have no understanding of what you have spoken. If God has used you to speak about some delicate matter, your understanding of it might be very embarrassing to the person/s involved. The Lord may give you the message in a way that you understand nothing but the person who is receiving the message understands all of it. In this way, everyone's interests are served.

Trust God. He knows what He is doing.

Encourage Those
Who Receive Prophecy To Obey

It is important to encourage the person receiving a prophecy to obey. In 1970, I traveled for nine months in ministry for the Lord, 55,000 miles by air and 15,000 miles by land, nearly circling the globe twice.

And I did it because of a prophetic word. Someone prophesied over me and mentioned ministry in the Marshalls, the Gilberts, the Hebrides, and named many of the other obscure islands of the Pacific.

God spoke of Colombo "where the palm trees would be waving in the breeze." When we approached Colombo (in former Ceylon), six or eight months later, the plane had difficulty landing because of the fierce winds and the airport was surrounded by Palm trees swaying in the breeze. And the rest of the prophecy was fulfilled in detail, as well.

We were raised to believe that God will honor us if we are foolish enough to launch forth on the word He has spoken to us through His prophets. Not everyone has been taught as well as we were.

When God tells me to run, I run. When He says, "Jump," I jump. If the Spirit of God directs me to give, I give. If He directs me to go, I go. I have learned that if I will obey Him, something wonderful will happen. And I am obligated to teach others the same.

Obedience is not always easy. When God spoke to me to go to all those islands, I found that it was very expensive to travel to some of them. To get to the Gilbert Islands, for instance, I had to go by way of Fiji, then 1,400 miles north and then turn around and come back the same way. There was no other alternative. The round trip ticket from Fiji was more than $400, and that was in 1970. Four hundred dollars was still a lot of money in those days. If I had not heard from God on the subject, I might have thought there were better ways to spend $400. It was a sacrifice for me, but I went because God had specifically named those places, so I knew it was His will for me to go.

In the Gilbert Islands, they had not had a visitor to the church in more than two years, and none of the members had received the Holy Ghost. God sent an outpouring of His Spirit, and how glad I was that I obeyed!

Let us encourage others, by sharing our own stories of victory and blessing, to obey God when He speaks to them through us. Do it any way that you can, but encourage people to respond, to act.

When God speaks of healing, encourage those who could not walk to start walking, to start moving the part of their body that was unmovable, to start doing what they couldn't do before God spoke.

If God is speaking to someone to travel in ministry, encourage them to take some step of faith, to pack a bag, to make time in their schedule for what God has spoken, to get a passport. Teach everyone that if they sit down and do nothing with the word God has given them, they are guaranteeing that nothing will happen.

Noah had to start building an ark. Moses had to tell the people to keep their shoes on all night to be ready to march early in the morning. Get the people moving. Get them to respond.

Many times the first step is up to us, and we will not see the hand of God until we first make a move. And if we never make a move, nothing will happen.

Some people come to me wanting to hear from God. I am led to ask them if they did what God told them to do the last time I prayed for them. If they say no, I ask why they want to hear more when they are not willing to do the first things God has spoken. God tells some people the same thing over and over because they haven't done it the first time He spoke to them.

Teach people that if they do what God tells them to do, He will speak to them again. If they do what He has already told them to do, He will speak something new to them the next time.

Encourage people to respond to God.

Don't Worry About Opposition

As the prophets of old faithfully delivered their message, there were always people standing by who branded them false and offered a more palatable message. We do not speak what people want to hear, but what God wants to say. Therefore, expect opposition and don't worry about it when it comes.

When God is using you, you simply can't be concerned about what anyone else thinks of it. If you do, you will lose your gift.

Once, when I was in Australia, God was moving in a wonderful way. Grown men who had been all their lives in Pentecost, but who had grown cold, were being stirred by the things God was saying to them, and we were experiencing revival. Then one day, I noticed two men with clipboards sitting at the back

of the service. They were making notes on everything that was going on, trying to find anything at all
to criticize. I just ignored them because I was determined not to stop what God was doing.

When you have fasted and prayed and you know
that you are hearing from God, don't worry about
what someone else may think or say. There will always be nay sayers, and if you pay attention to them,
you will get nothing accomplished.

You walk in the fear of God and you can be sure
that what you are speaking is God. And when He
brings the confirmation of what you are saying, others will realize it also. Do things in a proper way,
always be in order, and leave it to God to judge your
critics. He is a better judge than you could ever be.

- 6 -

How Can You Encourage
Your Members to Prophesy?

There are several reasons that we have so few people who prophesy in our churches these days. The first reason more of our members are not prophesying is that they have not been taught on the subject and are, therefore, hesitant to step out into something they don't understand. So, the first thing we need to do in all our churches to get more people prophesying is to teach more about the gifts of the Spirit.

Teach More About the Gifts

The more we learn about prophecy, the more confidence we can have in its use. This is true of anything. We need much more teaching in our local churches to make people aware of what we can and should be doing in the prophetic realm and how it is to be done.

I find myself teaching on this vital subject at least one morning in every crusade I conduct. In our campmeetings, there are always some new people who have limited knowledge of the role of prophets and prophecy in the Church today and who are eager to move into new things in God, and since prophecy is one of my favorite themes, I often preach and teach about it.

How can our people move into things that they don't know exist? How can they appropriate promises that they don't know are their's? If you don't teach your children something, you can't blame them later for not knowing it. And we cannot blame our members for what we are not teaching them.

We need much more teaching concerning the things of the Spirit.

When I was in Iowa a few years ago, and began to minister to the people in prophecy, the pastor said to me, "It wouldn't bother me if you didn't preach while you are here. We have never seen prophecy like this and I would prefer that you take the time to obey God in this respect." And that man had been preaching for twenty years.

As we ministered to the people who were attending, some were getting saved, some were being healed, others were being filled with the Spirit of God, while others were receiving new direction for their lives. And during several nights of that crusade I did not preach because there were so many people who had serious needs that required our immediate attention.

On several other nights of that particular series of meetings, I probably shouldn't have preached. I felt constrained to do it to avoid the criticism of those who say we are replacing the word of God with prophecy. But God was moving in such a way that we could have omitted the preaching of the Word and all been blessed and edified.

At least one man was offended by the absence of the preaching. He came to me and asked, "Can you preach?"

I wasn't offended by the question. "I do," I said, "when the need arises." I knew that God had been doing wonderful things in the lives of those people, and I wasn't going to let the attitude of someone who didn't understand what God was doing change that.

The principle reason that pastor had never seen God move in that way and had never prophesied in more than twenty years of ministry was that he had received no teaching on the subject. After I had taught on prophecy, he moved into a wonderful prophetic ministry.

The more we teach our people about the gifts of the Spirit, the more it becomes second nature to them, the more they lose their fear of the supernatural, and the more ready they are to launch out into the operation of the gifts.

We need to understand the purpose of the gifts, we need to understand the proper timing of the gifts, and we need to feel comfortable in the operation of the gifts.

Teaching people about prophecy is just as important as teaching a child to walk and is done in much the same manner. Left alone, some children would eventually learn to walk on their own, but it would take much longer and many would never learn. We first show them that it is possible, we encourage them to do it and we help them get started. If no one tells us we can prophesy, we don't know we can and may never try.

Teach your people about the availability of the gifts of the Spirit to every believer.

Give People An Opportunity

The greatest reason the average member of the church never prophesies is that he or she is never given an opportunity. It is one thing to talk about prophecy or to study prophecy, but it is quite another thing to actually start prophesying. All that study may accomplish nothing — if it is not put into practice.

Many church leaders are afraid to let their members prophesy for fear of letting the service get out of hand. "How can you keep order in a service if people are free to do what they want?" they reason.

Well, that is the purpose of leadership, to keep everything flowing in the proper order. But God never intended for all ministry to be in the hands of a few. He has given us a Body ministry and has placed a variety of gifts in a variety of members of that Body — for the benefit of the whole Body.

If the leaders of a church are prayerful and are themselves moving in the Spirit of God, they should have no difficulty in maintaining the proper order in the service and seeing that everything flows together for the benefit of all.

In our own congregation, we not only encourage everyone to prophesy, we prepare for it. We keep microphones with long chords ready at all times to be whisked to any person who stands to give a word from the Lord. We want everyone to hear what God is saying, and we want to record what is being said so that we can later go back and listen to it again and pick up anything we missed.

In doing this, we feel that we are honoring the Spirit of God by honoring those that He is using. And, He honors us with His presence, as a result.

In some large churches, prophecy becomes a problem because of the need for everyone to hear what is being said. Often the decision is made that everything will come from the platform. That may be fine in some cases, where everyone on the platform is anointed and moving in God. But, in the end, it cannot be good for the whole congregation. How will the others learn? How will the others grow? We prefer to keep microphones available so that God can use the persons He chooses, not those that we chose.

Some churches limit prophecy to the leadership which customarily sits on the platform. Others limit the privilege of prophecy to board members. Others, while more open, say that you must be a member of their church to be recognized for prophecy. Some of the charismatic churches, because of their need to balance the moving of the Spirit with the more traditional aspects of the church, limit prophecy to certain services. And, of course, in many other churches prophecy is considered unacceptable in any form.

Who gave us the right to place such limitations on the Holy Ghost? These are not our gifts. They are gifts *of* the Spirit. That word 'of' denotes possession. These are His gifts, and He reserves the right to manifest them when and where and through whom He wishes.

One church sets aside a three day period each year as a special prophecy conference. During that time, they invite those who are considered to have a special gift of prophecy to come together, fast and pray, and then minister to their people.

I am glad they have such a conference. But I am sad for them that the other 362 days of the year they and their people are robbed of this wonderful blessing. God did not set this gift and its corresponding ministry into a three-day convention. He set it into the Body for its edification — 365 days a year.

God said, *"Ye may all prophesy."* And He meant it.

Some pastors are so afraid of losing control of their services to someone who may prophesy that they sing down the prophesies or have the person prophesying physically sat down or even taken out.

In our church, no one is ever sat down in anger by our leadership. We wouldn't want to risk generating fear in any of God's children. Those who are afraid cannot know the moving of the Spirit of God. They will remain *ignorant concerning spiritual gifts.*

Those who are in leadership have the responsibility to understand the mind of the Spirit and be able to guide the service in the way that is pleasing to God. We are not called to *quench* the Spirit:

> *Quench not the Spirit.*   1 Thessalonians 1:1

We are called to direct the service as would be beneficial to all, and that means encouraging the participation of more of God's children; for we all have something to offer.

The gifts of the Spirit should be flowing in such a way today as to convince the people around us that God is indeed with us and is helping us. We must never be ashamed of what God has done and of what He is doing. This world needs to know that God is alive.

When a modern-day prophet comes along (those who use the powers of the devil to try to predict the future), they receive great publicity. For many years Jean Dixon appeared regularly in the tabloid newspaper headlines, in respected newspapers, and on television and radio. Her books sold millions of copies, and she was quoted on regular news broadcasts. Many politicians and other pop figures of the day have regularly looked to her for advice.

Those who deal in clairvoyance, hypnosis, mental telepathy, fortune telling, and others of the black arts all say that they get their power from God and that their revelations are inspired of God. Ask any fortune teller. She will tell you that God has given her the unusual power she possesses. And thousands are being deceived by these people.

The reason is that the world is starving for the true manifestations of God and are quickly taken in by those who only imitate His power. Fortune tellers are just a counterfeit, a phony copy of that which you and I should be flowing in as spirit-filled believers. We need the move of God in our congregations.

Some churches are afraid to allow the gifts of the Spirit to operate for fear of what they call "wildfire." I have no idea what they are talking about because I have been in Pentecost for more than thirty years and I haven't seen it yet. The problem is not wildfire, it is no fire. By constantly warning people about wildfire, we are only sowing fear and doubt concerning the works of God's Spirit.

The problem many times is that the very leaders of the church don't understand the moving of the Spirit of God well enough to bring the service into that flow. If we are spirit-filled, then we ought to know what the Spirit is saying and doing. Then we can throw away the program and let the Spirit of God work in our midst.

If you have a sense of security in the Holy Ghost yourself, you won't be so concerned about things getting out of hand. Encourage your people to worship in the Spirit, to walk in the Spirit, to develop the fruit of the Spirit and to move in the gifts of the Spirit.

More than 2,000,000 ouïja boards are sold annually in America. Witchcraft, sorcery and psychic reading are all making strong comebacks. And the most popular page in most American newspapers is the one containing the horoscopes. While our Pentecostal churches sit back, worrying that something will get out of hand, people all over our country are turning to the black arts to try to find answers to their problems.

If we would dare to stand in the power of God and declare His counsel, we would see Him work just as in the days of the great prophets of old and crowds would be drawn to our churches again.

A man involved in psychic phenomena came to our area, and I was asked to go talk with him. I challenged him. "I don't have to read Jean Dixon's predictions to know what will happen in the days ahead," I told him. "God is speaking to us by His Spirit. And if you want to find out what is happening, come and sit in some of our meetings and listen to the Holy Ghost reveal coming events to us."

The excitement of the hour should be in the house of God. We should be drawing reporters to our doors. Stop holding back for fear that a little flesh will get involved. Let God have His way.

Give opportunity to your members to prophesy. Don't just jump from song to song, and program to program. It is often good to encourage people to prophesy the first day they receive the Holy Ghost. That will get them off to a very good start.

Be Patient With the Little Ones

When anyone is just beginning to prophesy, they may make some mistakes. That would be only normal. Create an atmosphere where no one feels inhibited and no one feels embarrassed when they don't do their best the very first time. We can all learn by our mistakes and grow so that we do better the next time.

A member who is not as spiritual as others but who is putting forth an effort to grow in God should not be excluded from the privilege of prophesying. Their prophecy may lack depth and anointing, but it is valid nevertheless. You don't have to be a Christian for fifty years before you begin to prophesy. The simplicity that such people project is exactly what many people need and are looking for. They are like children in many ways. They lack guile. They have not yet been tainted with all the church scandals, splits, and jealousies. God can use them.

When a baby first begins to walk, it may fall down many times. It would be unusual if it didn't fall some. If the mother would scold the child every time it fell down, it might stop trying and never learn to walk. God has not called us to put down those who are trying to learn to operate in the gifts of the Spirit. If they are out of order in some way, or if they have missed the proper timing, we can help them in a loving way that will encourage them to get back up and try again.

If a person doesn't take good correction and seems to want to take over the church and do things in their own way, then we must become more stern with them as with any unresponsive child. But don't be guilty of quenching the enthusiasm of those who are beginning and sincerely want to learn to prophesy.

Don't wait until your people are perfect before you give them an opportunity; for if they have no opportunity to begin, they can never become perfected.

Being used in prophecy does something wonderful for any believer. When any of us is more greatly used of God than in times past, a new excitement comes to our soul. It causes us to seek the face of God and move to a new spiritual level in Him. If all we are doing week after week is sitting on the church pew, there is not much incentive to strive for the deeper spiritual life.

You may not be impressed with your members and may not think they have much potential. But God knows better. If you would get close and over-hear what He is saying to some of them, your opinions of them and their potential for the future might suddenly change. You may have looked upon that individual as limited in talent and possibility, but when you hear God's great plan for them, you may be convinced that you were wrong. Then you will be encouraged to make every effort to help them achieve what God has promised.

If God said they can do it, then they can do it.

If God said it would happen, then it will happen.

If God said, He would do it, He will do it.

Be patient with the little ones, and one day soon they will have grown into spiritual giants.

If two people in diverse parts of the building begin to prophesy at the same time, they may not be able to hear each other and will continue speaking at the same time. In this case, someone sitting or standing beside one of those people should simply touch them, drawing their attention to the other speaker so that they can prefer them. If one or the other is a more mature believer, it is actually better for the more mature one to stop and prefer the other because they are less likely to be embarrassed or offended in that situation.

If two children are doing the same thing, we usually ask the older one to allow the baby to have the experience first. Because the older one is more mature, he or she will usually be understanding and give the younger one first turn.

Be patient with the little ones.

Avoid Sowing Fear

Some people have taught that it is possible for the devil to speak through a spirit-filled Christian, and this has put great fear into their hearts. The Bible is very clear on this point:

> *Ye cannot drink the cup of the Lord, and the cup of devils: ye cannot be partakers of the Lord's table, and of the table of devils.*
>
> 1 Corinthians 10:21

You CANNOT! So when I prophesy something strange, something that I don't understand and the people I am prophesying to don't understand, I never entertain the thought that it might be from the devil. NEVER! I just wait on God to give me understanding of what has been spoken. It cannot be from the devil for I am a born-again, spirit-filled child of God.

The devil can oppose you. He can oppress you and fight against you. But unless you renounce your faith and get on his side, he cannot take control of your life. He cannot possess you. You belong to God.

Those who teach that believers can prophesy words inspired of Satan are spreading a spirit of fear and God has said:

> *For ye have not received the spirit of bondage again to fear; but ye have received the Spirit of adoption, whereby we cry, Abba, Father.*
> Romans 8:15

We are not called to propagate fear. Faith and fear are opposites. Faith is of God and fear is of the devil. God controls His people through faith, while Satan controls his people through fear. The two can never mix. Lay aside all fear yourself, and avoid sowing fear in the hearts of others.

One of the things I work hard to do in our meetings is to make people comfortable in the exercise of the gifts of the Spirit, to remove all their fears. This is the reason we have many who exercise these gifts well.

When you sow fear in people's hearts, by telling them, "We believe in the moving of the Spirit of God, but just be sure that it's God," you are hindering God's people from moving forward.

If you keep telling a child about the dangers of falling and how badly they can hurt and embarrass themselves, they will be afraid to try to take the first steps. Yes, the danger is there. But you are there to catch them if they start to fall, so you tell them not to worry about falling, just to start walking.

The same is true with prophecy. Don't sow fear in people's hearts about all the possible dangers. Encourage them to just start walking. And if you are a mature person, guide them away from pitfalls and places where they might fall. That's your job — not to discourage them from even trying.

Allow Time For God to Work

One of the greatest hindrances to the operation of the gifts of the Spirit in our churches today is the time constraints. The press of activities and heavy schedules of our leaders and our members has caused us to get in too much of a hurry. But God is not in a hurry. There are needy people in our services, and God wants to meet their need.

If necessary, we should forget about the special music we have planned, so that God may have time to move by His Spirit. Some of the music being performed in churches today doesn't add anything to the anointing of the service anyway, so it wouldn't hurt to shorten it or omit it altogether. Do whatever is necessary to give the Spirit time to work.

Don't keep looking at the clock. I was in a service in North Carolina once when those in charge were about to dismiss the people. I sensed, however, that God was not finished with us and asked them to wait a little longer in the presence of the Lord, praising Him and anticipating His blessing.

Before long, a man who had lost his sight nine years before because of a destroyed optic nerve began to see. He was slain in the Spirit. Several people were filled with the Spirit for the first time. A boy that was paralyzed from the neck down began to have sensations of feeling throughout his body, and the entire group of people were rejoicing in God. It was nearly midnight when we left the place, but we all knew that we had been with God.

If we make no time available to God, how can He speak to us? In a church service there should be times when God can speak to us in prophecy. If we allocate no time for Him, can we complain that He doesn't speak in these days?

We cannot control God or tell Him when to move, but we can take time not to rush through the worship service, to let the people linger in the presence of God for some moments, giving God the opportunity He needs to speak to us, as He desires.

The operation of the gifts of the Spirit are just as important a part of the service as the preaching, the prayer, or the offering. Make time for them.

Avoid Jealousies

Some well-known ministers will never tell you how to prophesy as they do. They don't want you to know, because if many people are doing it, they reason, it will take all the mystery out of prophecy, and they and their ministries will be diminished. But they are wrong. God said, *"All may prophesy,"* and that doesn't diminish anyone.

It is time we looked beyond the well-being of our own ministries and began to concern ourselves more with the well-being of the entire Body of Christ. Any body part that is not exercised becomes limp and useless and we the entire body suffers as a result.

We need more people with the gift of prophecy in these days. A few are not enough. How are we to have more people operating the gifts if we fall into petty jealousies over their use. God is raising up a new generation of believers to go forth and conquer for Him. Don't hinder that new generation by your reluctance to allow competition in your area of ministry.

If you know the Lord and understand His mind, you should have no fear that someone will bypass you and outshine you in the gifts. Maturity takes away all those insecurities. Your son is not a threat to you. Encourage him to walk. His walking will not diminish you as a person.

The parent who doesn't want his or her child to walk for fear of that walking diminishing their own importance and prominence is not a person of love.

We are not diminished when others do well. To the contrary, since we are all part of the same family, what another does well blesses all of us.

The fact that God begins to use a younger believer in the church in the gift of healing doesn't diminish the role or the respect of the pastor. That's the way it ought to work. If we are imparting nothing, and if our people are not moving into ministry themselves, we are failures. Satan has warped our sensibilities and caused us to think wrong thoughts. Let us get the entire body involved in the things of the Spirit. That is success.

Don't get jealous of the gifts of another, especially your own children. There is strength in numbers. There is strength in having more people involved. It is so beautiful when pieces of revelation come through many to form an entire picture when it is all put together. *Ye may all prophesy.*

I have had pastors say to me very sincerely, "Brother Heflin, you are killing our ministries. If you tell our people that they can all operate the gifts of the Spirit, what is left for us to do?" But that is foolish thinking. There is plenty for all of us to do and the more hands we put to the task, the greater area of the harvest field we will be able to reap for the Lord.

As our members move into the gifts, this challenges us as pastors to rise up to new heights of revelation and exercise of gifts for our own ministries. Because we have children who are doing well doesn't diminish us as a person. If we are constantly moving into new areas of wisdom, our children will always recognize us as their spiritual parents. But we can do so much more with the children working than we can if it is only one or two working.

In a given crusade, I may be content to do all the prophesying the first few nights, but before long, I want to get others involved — for two reasons: (1.) So that we can do more for God during the crusade or revival meeting and (2.) So that the ministry of prophecy will continue after I have gone on to other places

In every place, I want to develop a small army of eight or ten or fifteen who have moved into the exercise of this gift so that the previous vacuum will not continue when I am gone. That does not diminish my own ministry in any way.

I get that small group to stand with me around the altar each service with the hungry ones who have come for ministry, and I want to see those who are willing move into the depths of prophecy. I am positive that I accomplish as much by encouraging them as I do by prophesying myself.

When I leave a place, I have a good feeling that the things God wants to do these days will continue in that place.

Get rid of your ministerial jealousies and encourage all of God's people to develop their full potential.

In our own ministry, when we have an outside speaker ministering in our church or camp or conferences, we feel it is better to allow them to do the prophetic ministry. Coming from outside, they may have some new insight.

When that minister has concluded his part of the service, if we feel that God is not finished with us yet, we call many of the people who have begun to move out in the gifts forward to pray over the people and minister to them. In this way, we have honored those whom God sends our way.

When no outside speaker is present, we are not under these constraints.

We cannot afford ministerial jealousy. It will rob us every time.

How Can You Claim
Your Prophetic Promises?

Each of us, as recipients of many wonderful prophetic promises, needs to claim all the words that have been spoken over us in the past. There are several things that I have found helpful in this regard.

Listen To It

It is impossible to claim a promise if you didn't even listen carefully to it and if you are not at all sure of what God said. We should encourage respect for the gifts of the Spirit and exercise respect ourselves, listening carefully so that we can later act on what we have heard. And you can't act on something you didn't hear.

Often God sets the tone for a particular service through a prophecy that is given early in that service. And often God gives us other specific instructions in a prophecy. We must learn to listen and assimilate what He is saying.

In any position of responsibility, we must be good listeners in order to carry out our duties. How can we justify not listening carefully to what God is saying to us?

Never allow prophecy to become so commonplace that you give it little attention.

Learn not only to listen carefully, but to listen carefully to every word. Reader's Digest Books tried to make a condensed version of the Bible. But when they finish taking a word out here and a phrase out here, it was left without power and no one liked it.

Every single word recorded in the Bible is important and has a purpose. Every *and* in the Bible is important. Every *if* in the Bible is important. And, in the same way, the things that God speaks in prophecy are important — down to the smallest word. Listen carefully to what God says. Every word has a meaning.

Remember It

Being a good listener will help us remember what we have heard. The message may be for a moment from now, for an hour later, for tomorrow, for next week or even for a year from now. Obviously, in the emotion of the moment, we can miss some of the details of the message, so there are several things we can do to help us remember.

The availability of cassette recorders has been a great blessing to those of us who believe in prophecy because we can listen to the prophecy again later to catch any details that may have escaped us the first time we heard it. Because of this, we record every prophecy that is given in our services.

When we feel that a certain prophecy has been especially important for the future, we ask someone to transcribe it and we keep it in printed form either in the Bible or somewhere close at hand where we can refer to it when the need arises. I have several on my desk at any given moment.

If you are somewhere that you don't have access to a recorder, write down the major points of the prophecy and keep them somewhere that you can review them from time to time. This is important to help you understand what God is saying.

Understand It

Many times we don't fully understand what God is saying to us. We may think we do, but as time goes on and we continue to ponder the message, we realize that it means something different from what we originally understood.

Just as there are parts of the Bible that we don't understand without periods of meditation and prayer, there are personal messages from God that don't seem to make sense to us — at the time. Or, if they do make sense, we understand them only in a limited way. Having those messages written down, at least the major points of them, will help immensely in the effort to understand, through prayer and meditation, exactly what God is saying to us.

Just as we understand, little by little, the mysteries of the Bible, the written Word of God, God is faithful to make known to us the meaning of the prophetic promises He gives us from day to day — if we wait upon Him for that understanding.

Remind Yourself of It

There are three persons that I must regularly remind about the promises of God given to me.

First, I must remind myself. This encourages my faith in difficult times and gives me direction for the days ahead.

Secondly, I must remind Satan. That robs him of his ability to control me and puts him in his proper place.

And, third, I must remind God. When He knows that I am holding on to His promises and refuse to let them fall to the ground, it shows Him my seriousness and my trust in His eventual fulfillment of every single word.

I refuse to let even one of those promises slip. I regularly bring them up in prayer, for I never know if this may be the time that God will bring one or more of them to pass.

I will admit that there are promises that I still don't fully understand, after quite some time. But I don't fret over those. I leave them to God's care.

I absolutely refuse to drop from my remembrance promises that seem unusual or beyond the realm of possibility. I remind God; I remind myself; and I remind the devil. Regularly rehearsing these in my spirit lets me know that the best days are yet to come and my faith is released.

God said to Moses:

> *Write this for a memorial in a book, and rehearse it in the ears of Joshua: for I will utterly put out the remembrance of Amalek from under heaven.*
>   Exodus 17:14

Whatever you need to do to remind yourself of what God has promised, do it.

Believe For It

Just as all the promises of the Bible are appropriated by faith, every prophetic promise is ultimately appropriated by faith. If you believe it and act upon it, God will do what He has promised.

When God said, *"Let there be light,"* nothing could stop the fulfillment of that word. And God did not stop until it was performed. The word He has given you is just as sure. Demons cannot stop it. Evil people cannot stop it. Only your own lack of faith and obedience can stop it.

Do not be discouraged. And stop wondering how it will all come to pass. Just start rejoicing in it and acting upon it.

Sometimes the word God gives us is overwhelming. It is far beyond our present level of faith, and we have to do some serious praying to bring our faith up the level of the promise God has given. Some years from now, we may look back and laugh at our immaturity. But right now that promise seems larger than Caleb's mountain.

To claim that promise, we have to start thinking differently. We have to start thinking God's thoughts. And when we start thinking differently, we can start talking differently. And when we start talking differently, we can start acting differently. And when we start acting differently, we can move into what God has prepared for us.

If your mind is overwhelmed by what God has said, let him renew your mind. Know that the blessing God has promised is on the way. Believe for it! Accept it! Anticipate it! Plan for it!

Some are so accustomed to receiving the manna of the wilderness that they cannot accept that God now wants to give them the corn from their own land.

Hear the voice of God and obey what He is telling you. Take it by faith. Start acting upon what God has spoken to you. Don't be afraid. And He will surely bring it to pass.

If you have a word from the Lord about going somewhere, that's all you need. You don't need to worry about transportation. You don't have to worry about where you will sleep. You don't have to wonder if you will have enough to eat. Get a word, and you can go forth on the basis of that word.

Peter got out of the boat and started walking because of one word from the Lord: *"Come."* He didn't ask HOW? He wasn't worried about HOW LONG it would take him. He wasn't thinking about WHAT would happen if he failed. Jesus said, "Come," and that was enough for Peter.

Jesus didn't say, "If you will get out of the boat, I will harden the water beneath your feet and keep you safe as you walk toward me." He said, "Come." He didn't say, "Don't worry, Peter, I can take care of you." He said, "Come." And that was enough.

The same word of God that spoke the worlds into existence will sustain you from day to day and take you forth into the perfect will of God for your life — if you will believe it and act upon it.

God's word will not let you down. It will not fail you.

If you let the word fall to the ground and refuse to claim it as your own, God is not obligated to fulfill it.

In the Bible, God has said:

I am the Lord that healeth thee.   Exodus 15:26

But if you don't appropriate that promise and claim it as your own, you will stay sick. God keeps His promises to those who believe Him. Many people have been sick for years because they have not believed that Exodus 15:26 is for them. The day you realize that it is your promise, you will be healed.

Your lack of faith hinders God. He cannot act on your behalf if you refuse to believe Him.

We are all waiting for God to fulfill His part of the contract, when, in reality, He is waiting for us to fulfill our part of the bargain. He is more than ready to act on our behalf.

If I would receive a prophetic word today that said, "Take a trip around the world," I would begin packing and be ready to leave on a moment's notice. I wouldn't need any other confirmation. I have done it. I know that God will bring to pass everything that He has spoken to me in prophecy.

If God tells you, "the struggles will cease," stand on that promise and expect every struggle to cease, just as He has said.

One summer, God spoke to me several times about His desire to prosper me. So, I just began to plan for prosperity, to change my way of thinking about my needs, my bills and my ministry. And God honored it.

I believe that a portion of every prophetic word that comes forth to the congregation is for each of us, not necessarily all of it, but a portion. If each of us will take that portion and hold on to it, God will move heaven and earth to bring it to pass in our lives.

Persevere

The greatest demonstration of our faith in the promises of God should be our perseverance. We will not be denied.

You can bank on the word of God. Write it down. Keep it with your Bible. Meditate on it and don't let one single word of it fall to the ground. And when the devil tries to tell you that it is not of God, chase him away without ceremony and cling to the promise you have received. God will honor the prophetic word in the same way He honors His written Word.

If you have traveled to a distant place and have received there a promise from God, at the same moment He is promising you what He will do, He is already at work on the other end of the situation. When you arrive home, or when you arrive at the office, or when you arrive at your destination, you will find that things have begun to change for the better — because the word of the Lord is sure.

Things are so different than you left them at times that you may wonder if you are in the same house. You may wonder if you are in the same office. You may wonder if you are around the same people, doing the same things. God can change your situation in a moment.

A sister from North Carolina prayed twelve years for her husband to get saved. One day, when she came in the door from visiting our camp, her husband told her that he wanted to get saved.

She couldn't believe her ears.

"What did you say?" she asked, just to be sure.

"I said I want to get saved, and if you can't help me, I'll go to Virginia and get Brother Heflin to help me," he answered. He was serious.

The two of them knelt together, and as he got saved, she felt like she was getting saved all over again. If you persevere, God will answer.

If God promises revival, revival will come. If He promises to change your loved ones, they will be changed. If He tells you to travel the nations for His glory, He will make a way for you to do it. If God tells you that you will stand before large groups of people and minister His Word, He will help you to do it. Believe it, get ready for it, and persevere in your faith in God's promise.

You may be preaching to a small handful now, but don't become discouraged. Your day is coming. Get ready for it. Be a part of what God is doing all over the world.

Everything you have gone through in the past has just been preparation for what God has for you today and tomorrow. The trials and troubles you have gone through have been to stretch you and prepare you for enlargement. Don't despise those hardships and difficulties. God allowed them all — for your good. They have prepared you for the anointing God is giving you today and for the miracles He is about to do for you and through you. Don't be discouraged. Don't sit back in despair. Don't give up now. Know that God has His hand upon you and that His word will never fail. His promises are sure.

Part II:

Ezekiel As Our Example

- 8 -

A Prophet At Work

Studying the book of Ezekiel through the years, I have found that the experiences of this prophet help us to understand what prophecy is and what it does. Reading Ezekiel, therefore, is to see a prophet at work.

The fact that Ezekiel was an Old Testament prophet doesn't hinder me in this regard since I know that God hasn't changed and wants to speak to His people today, just as He did thousands of years ago.

The Valley of Dry Bones

Ezekiel was sent to a cemetery to prophesy. In many old Middle Eastern cemeteries, the bodies were not buried. They were placed in tombs above the ground. Somehow the bodies that Ezekiel confronted that day had been exposed to the elements.

The birds had come and eaten the flesh until nothing but bones remained. And then the sun had baked the bones until they were bleached and white — and dry.

Rather than an actual cemetery, this may have been the site of some ancient battle. That would explain why the bodies were scattered about. Perhaps they had never been properly buried. Whatever the case, God had a work for His prophet to do in this most unusual place.

The Hand of the Lord Was Upon Me

Ezekiel was an acceptable prophet because *the hand of the Lord was upon* him. Don't approach just anyone and ask them to give you a word from God. They might tell you anything. Look for a person who has the touch of God upon his life. Some people are so eager to receive a prophecy that they seek it from anybody and everybody, and that is dangerous. Be sure that the hand of God is upon the person who prophesies over you.

You cannot be a true prophet, and you cannot prophesy effectively unless you have been touched by *the hand of the Lord.* I would rather have the touch of God on my life than to be a millionaire. If I was a millionaire, the stock market could drop fifteen or twenty points, and I could lose a major part of my investment overnight. But because *the hand of the Lord* is upon my life, I have something that no amount of money can buy, and no one can steal it from me either.

When God's touch is upon your life, when He walks with you and talks with you, it places upon you a responsibility toward others. It was this responsibility that made Ezekiel willing to be carried away by the Spirit of the Lord.

And [He] Carried Me Out In the Spirit

Ezekiel was carried away by the Spirit of the Lord, and if you and I will allow ourselves to be carried away by the Spirit, we will do some unusual things too, things that will bring glory to God and reveal His great power to others.

God's purpose in our lives is not to make us more comfortable so that we can enjoy the "good life." His purpose is to carry us out to the dry bones of this world. I get invitations from churches that are on fire and moving in God, but I often feel that they don't really need my help. They are doing fine without me. I want to go to those valleys full of dry bones where I know I am needed.

If ministers only go to churches that are already moving in God, their invitations will be limited. Go where you are needed, and don't be afraid to go where the bones are very dry.

You may only have one night or two nights to get dry bones to come to life, and you can't do that by yourself. Only the Spirit of God can do such a work. But He will do it — if the hand of the Lord is upon you and if you will allow yourself to be carried away by the Spirit.

When God opens a door of ministry to you, never feel that you are in a certain place only because you had a free night. Never feel that you are there only because you needed money. If God has brought you to a place, He has a higher purpose for your being there. Someone there needs your touch. Someone there needs your word.

This need places upon each of us, as servants of God, a great responsibility to stay in a place of constant fellowship and communion with Him, so that we can bring His life to those whom we meet everywhere. We cannot go into a place and give the people the same thing we fed people in the last place we were. We must have the right word for each place and for each person.

Sometimes, when we are carried away by the Spirit, it is for the purpose of helping us arrive on time at some important scene. Philip had this experience. At other times, the carrying away is to bring us to a place of greater vision. Some are carried away into Heaven, while others actually visit the pits of Hell. Others may visit some place on the earth. Ezekiel was privileged to visit a cemetery, a place of dry bones.

And [He] Set Me Down in the Midst of the Valley Which Was Full of Bones

"What a hard place!" some preachers say. "What a dry place!" Yes, that's why God has brought you there. And if you have some life to offer to dry bones, the Lord will consistently carry you to them so that you can do what God has called you to do. We all like to fellowship with on-fire people, but we need to go sometimes to the dead ones so that we can share with them the life Jesus has given us.

If the fire is already burning, all a church needs is for someone to fan the flames. If, however, there is no flame, they need someone like you who can breathe life back into dead bones. Let the Spirit of God carry you out where men and women need what you are offering.

There is no lack of places to minister across our own country and around the world — if you are willing to be carried away in the Spirit to those who really need your help and to be set down in valleys full of dry bones.

Without the carrying away in the Spirit, without the anointing of the Spirit of God, we have nothing to offer and no reason to prophesy to dry bones. We cannot bring about change through our own efforts. But our God is life, and He can make dead bones live again. And we can do it too when His touch is upon us.

If you want God to use you, put yourself in the place that God can carry you away in the Spirit. Let Him carry you out of yourself into new depths of anointing. Let Him carry you out into greater revelation. Yield yourself to His purposes. Let Him set you down in the midst of the valley full of bones.

Don't be afraid. Don't be concerned about what you will do or what you will say. Revival is not the work of any man. Life-giving is beyond our ability to perform. Prophecy is not your responsibility. This is a miraculous gift of the Spirit of God. Let the Spirit carry you out to where men and women need to hear a word of life from their Creator.

And, Lo, They Were Very Dry

When Ezekiel looked at those bones, what he saw was not encouraging. They were *very dry*, and he was not at all sure that they could live again. But when something is *very dry*, it burns easily. Hallelujah! The souls that are difficult to set on fire are the half-wet/half-dry kind. When you try to get *them* burning, you usually just get a lot of smoke. When souls are dry, however, just a spark of the Holy Ghost can set them alight.

Don't worry about how dry things are. Just get yourself into the place that you are ready to light a spark of fire. God only needs one anointed prophet to turn a graveyard upside down.

If you only go where revival already exists, you might miss the greatest miracles God wants to do for you. If you only go where things are already happening, you might miss the excitement of igniting the fire and seeing it grow. Take some chances. Let the Spirit carry you out to those who are hungry for His love. Don't be afraid of dry bones.

And He Said Unto Me, Can These Bones Live?

When God told Ezekiel to prophesy to dead bones, he asked him the question: *Can these bones live?* When Ezekiel looked, he saw that the bones were bleached and dried by the sun. He noticed that they were all disconnected and scattered, one bone now having little relationship to others to which it had once been joined. So Ezekiel didn't know what to answer. He could only say: "Oh God, You know."

Some churches are so dead that you can feel the dryness when you walk in the door. It doesn't take you long to know that there is no life present in that place. Some traditional churches have a flame that burns constantly in the sanctuary. That fire is symbolic of the Holy Ghost. He wants to be burning in our midst always. But it isn't so in many churches.

"Can these bones live?"

"Lord, You are the only one who can say for sure if these dead things will ever come to life or not. You know."

It doesn't make any difference how dead things are. When the Spirit of God begins to move, death will turn to life, and that which before would not move will begin moving. Just prophesy to them. Say to them, 'Oh, ye dry bones, hear the Word of the Lord.'

Again He Said Unto Me, Prophesy Upon These Bones

Dry bones cannot come to life unless they hear God's anointed word. Telling people about your in-

sights and ideas will not move then. Telling people
about your children and grandchildren will not
move them. But when you begin to speak forth the
word of the Lord, those bones will begin to shake
and something unusual will happen. *Prophesy to
them.*

God is looking for men and women who will get
out of the rut, get out of the doldrums, get out of the
pattern of things they have been walking in now for
some time, and take a new step in the Spirit. Being
conservative is comfortable, and most churches like
being comfortable. They feel safe with the familiar.
Some churches have trained their deacons to approach anyone who does anything out of the
ordinary and quietly pray for them or lead them out
of the service if necessary. They don't feel comfortable with the unusual.

But our God is a God of variety and delights in
moving in a variety of ways. He desires to have pre-
eminence in every service, to do things in His way
and to, thus, receive all the glory for what is accomplished.

Don't be afraid of the new. Don't be afraid of the
different. If something is always the same, it may
mean that it has stopped growing, and that's dangerous.

When we are willing to be a vessel in the hands of
God, He will bless. He will do unusual things. God
says that He takes *the foolish things of the world to confound the wise*:

> *But God hath chosen the foolish things of the world to confound the wise; and God hath chosen the weak things of the world to confound the things which are mighty; And base things of the world, and things which are despised, hath God chosen, yea, and things which are not, to bring to nought things that are: That no flesh should glory in his presence.*   1 Corinthians 1:27-29

God is looking for those who will be willing to be His mouthpiece. John the Baptist was such a man. He couldn't take the credit for what God was doing. He was just *the voice*. But he also didn't have to worry about what he would say or where he would say it or how he would say it. He was just *the voice*. Prophecy is of God. He is the Source. We are just His voices.

So I Prophesied As I Was Commanded

What do you prophesy to dead bones? You don't need to tell them they are dead. They already know it. You need to tell them about the life they can have in God. You need to tell them what is possible. Ezekiel's word was positive:

> *I will cause breath to enter into you, and ye shall live. I will lay sinews upon you, and will bring up flesh upon you, and cover you with skin, and put breath in you, and ye shall live; and ye shall know that I am the Lord.*   Ezekiel 37:6

So the message we give is the message we have been commanded. And we give that message to the people we are commanded. When some people come to me and ask to be prayed for, I don't feel like doing it. If I know them or know something about them, I may not feel like God has much to say to them. But I am not the judge of that. So I just pray, and if I receive a word for them, I give that word. My ministry to them must not be limited by my personal feelings — if I happen to have any.

This is not your gift to choose when it will operate and who will receive a word from God. It is God's gift, and He will direct its operation.

Whether or not people can give something to God or to my ministry must have absolutely nothing to do with the operation of this gift. I must not be motivated by the thought of receiving something in exchange for a prophecy. That is not the purpose of the gift. If that were the case, we might only prophesy over the rich. But God loves us all — rich and poor alike and wants to speak to the poor just as much as He wants to speak to the rich. We cannot be influenced in our prophecy by the way a person is dressed.

We do not choose to minister or not to minister to a given person. Soon after I began preaching, God sent me to North Carolina for a crusade. I was fasting and praying and felt a great anointing for the services. I believed that everyone I laid hands on would be healed.

When I came back to Richmond, I encountered a man in our church who, after finishing his military service, had worked for the railroad, shoveling coal. He was tired of being covered with coal dust and was determined to get a disability pension from the military.

He would have each of us pray for him several times before each service ended. During the daytime, he would call us at home and have each of us pray for him. After a while, I felt that if I continued to pray for him, I was saying that God hadn't heard us the first time we prayed. And I was sure that he was just building a case for his disability pension. He didn't really want to be healed, and no matter how many times we prayed, he didn't receive it. He was just waiting for the day that he could be admitted to the hospital and begin his papers for the pension he wanted.

So I decided not to pray for him anymore. If I saw him approaching in one aisle of the church, I carefully made my way down another. If he moved over to that aisle, I found myself busy greeting someone on the other side. I went out one door, around to the back and in the back door, just to avoid that man. Then one day the Lord said to me, "Whose anointing is it? Yours? Or Mine?"

"It's Yours, Lord," I answered and knew that I had been severely rebuked of the Lord. It took me several months to recover the place of anointing I had been walking in, and through that lesson God taught me that His gifts are not mine to do with as I choose. I must work as I am commanded.

Now I am not offended by people like that, and there are always a few around. I will pray for them anytime and minister to them anytime. The gift is not mine, and I do not choose how it is used. Christ is Lord of the Church. I am His servant, and I will minister when and where and to whom He chooses.

Sometimes we grow weary ministering to long lines of people who are hungry for God. The more we pray the longer the line seems to get. And, when we have finished praying for everyone in the line and are looking for a place to sit down, another comes and requests prayer. It would be easy to say that we have no more time or no more strength. But while there are hungry souls, I cannot bring myself to do it.

I may be exhausted at times, but I know that God always has another word for someone who is standing by. There is always a little more oil remaining in the cruse. And the word for those who have waited will not be a lesser word than others have received. Indeed, God seems to outdo himself for those who have waited patiently their turn. And He has something very special to say to them. Since you are only the voice, the prophecy does not depend on your physical strength.

Prophesy as you are commanded.

As I Prophesied, There Was A Noise, and Behold A Shaking

God was ready to put life into dead bones, but Ezekiel had to do something too. He had to open his mouth and speak forth what God was showing him. He had to act. He had to obey.

You will not see miracles until you obey. You will not see deliverance until you act. God does His part, but you must first do your part. Prophesy. How can you know what God will do before you even make an effort to obey Him?

If God told Ezekiel to prophesy to dry bones, and those bones lived, you and I can prophesy to situations that need life in them. What could be more dead sometimes than our pocketbooks or our bank accounts? If Ezekiel could prophesy to dead bones, you can speak the word of the Lord to your aches and pains. I am convinced that we can prophesy to our own needs and our own situations as the Spirit of God moves upon us.

Many years ago a group of Australians and several from other countries came to America to minister. One day, while they were in the Carolinas, they were talking about their lack of finances. God told them to prophesy to their money. There were five or six of them, but when they had all laid their money on the table, they only had $42 between them.

Obeying God, they began to pray together and when the anointing was upon them, they began to prophesy. That week over $1,700 came into their hands, and they were able to continue their ministry in this country.

There is no situation too difficult for God to change. If you and I will hear the voice of the Lord for our situation, we can boldly speak forth His will into that situation and see it changed for the glory of God.

You can prophesy to your children to get saved. You can prophesy to your business to start prospering. If Ezekiel could tell dry bones to live, you can prophesy to empty things to be filled. You can prophesy to lost things to be found. You can prophesy to wounded things to be healed. You can prophesy to things that are sick to get well.

Prophesy over your home. Prophesy over your town. Prophesy over your state. Prophesy over your nation. Jeremiah did it, and you can too. If the word of life is flowing out of you, it will bring life and healing, fullness, and health. When God spoke and said, *"Let there be light,"* the creative force of His word brought light out of darkness. It brought light where there was no light. That word did not *return void.* And this is the promise of God.

That same creative power that was manifest in the formation of the worlds and everything that is found in them is still active in the prophetic word. All of heaven is behind God's word. The Godhead backs it up.

And when what you have spoken seems impossible, don't despair. God is still in the business of doing impossible things. If what you have spoken doesn't exist, then God will create it, for He has not lost His creative powers.

When you speak to a man to rise and walk, and his natural ability to walk is long ago dissipated by sickness or accident, God can make him walk again. When you speak to eyes that have not seen for a long time and have lost their natural ability to see, God can give them a miraculous ability to see.

One young man came to our church to preach over a period of many years. His eye had been removed when he was a child. But when he was prayed for, God allowed him to see — although there was no eyeball present. Teams of doctors examined him and declared it impossible for him to see. Yet, under the anointing he would tape over his good eye and read anything that was handed to him. And he did it through the socket of that missing eye. Whether his glass eye was in or out didn't make any difference. He could see through it. God can do what no other can do. And if dead bones can live, then dead eyes can see.

And the Bones Came Together

No sooner had Ezekiel spoken the words than something began to happen. There was *a noise*. There was a *shaking*. And bones began to come together.

When you move into the prophetic realm, something will begin to happen. Where there was no hope, hope will suddenly spring up. Where there was no life, you will see signs of life. Where there was an impossibility, suddenly you will see doors swinging open. You will see a change on people's faces, and you will see a change in their physical situation. When you take that step of faith, God be-

gins to move on your behalf. His creative word goes
to work on your behalf and changes things.

When I laid hands on a certain man, his head felt
like the hardest head I had ever placed my hand on.
God began to give me words for him, and I spoke
them forth:

> *You want them to come to you and ask your*
> *forgiveness, but I want you to go to them and*
> *ask their forgiveness.*
> *Those things that would not work, I will make*
> *them work.*
> *Those things that are rusted, I will oil. Those*
> *things that are dead, will receive new life.*

The message went on for about five minutes in this
vein. I was conscious, as I spoke and ministered to
him, that a woman had come up, put her arms
around him and begun weeping and praying.

When we got home to the pastors house that night,
he said to me, "You couldn't have understood what
God was doing tonight, but the wife of the man you
prayed for was having an affair with another man in
the church. Only a few of us had come to know about
it. I had made an appointment with them tomorrow
to try to deal with the situation. But tonight the Holy
Ghost put that man and his wife back together."

When I thought over the words of the prophecy, I
was amazed: "That which would not work, I will
make it work. That thing which is dead, I will put
new life in it."

If you obey God, look for some shaking, and don't be disturbed by the resulting noise. Expect bones to begin to come together.

Not every situation responds immediately. Sometimes things get worse before they get better. You have to be ready for that, too. But know that God is working and the end result will be a positive one.

Then He Said Unto Me, Prophesy Unto the Wind

It was bad enough to have to prophesy to dead bones. Now God told Ezekiel to stand in the middle of the field and prophesy to the wind. If someone would catch you doing that today, they would be sure you had lost your mind. But if God tells you to start prophesying to the wind, you had better start prophesying to the wind.

Long before Communism had failed, God spoke to two young men from Melbourne, Australia, to go stand in Red Square in Moscow and prophesy. They traveled to Russia, placed themselves in Red Square, faced Lenin's tomb, and raised their voices to declare the word of the Lord for Moscow. Part of their message was, "Thus saith the Lord: Let My people go." And hundreds of thousands of Jews have come out of Russia since that time. It works — when God is in it.

Prophesy to the wind. The wind carries whatever is committed to it. It has the power to spread it around, to scatter it here and there. Don't be afraid to prophesy to the wind.

You can prophesy to your dry church. You can prophesy to your dry family members. You can prophesy to your city. You can prophesy to your own situation. Let the wind carry your blessings far and wide.

When you start prophesying life to your church, some of the dead wood may have to be moved aside so that some living branches can start to grow. But God knows how to do it all.

Become bold. Get reckless. Believe God to move in your situation.

So I Prophesied As He Commanded Me

And when Ezekiel prophesied to the wind, something began to happen.

> *So I prophesied as he commanded me, and the breath came into them, and they lived, and stood up upon their feet, an exceeding great army.*
> Ezekiel 37:10

A few moments before there had been nothing there but some old parched and dried bones. They were useless in that form. They served no good purpose. But when someone with a touch of God upon his life began to speak the word of the Lord to those bones, they were transformed and turned into *an exceeding great army*. Hallelujah! That's the power of the word that is in your mouth. It will turn dead things into great and living things. And it can be done in a moment's time.

Prophecy breathes life into dead things. Prophesy, and see God work His miracles. Prophesy, and see God bring life to the dead things around you.

> *They lived.*
> *They stood.*
> *[They became] a great army.*

Praise God!

The prophetic word will breathe life into anyone it touches. It will place them on their feet. It will make them a viable part of God's great army. Prophecy lifts men and women out of despair and fills their hearts with joy and anticipation. It wipes away all vestiges of despondency and causes men and women to overflow with the blessings of the Most High God.

I have seen it happen time and time again. I have watched as God lifted great weights from people's shoulders and put them on a path to victory. I have watched as that dead, dry soul came to life and began to rejoice in the goodness of the Lord.

I have laid my hands on weak and failing ministers and seen them strengthened to stand in the power and glory of the Spirit. I have watched them as they then began to prophesy over their own people and turn *their* lives upside down, as well. Congregation after congregation has declared, "We have a new pastor." "He is a new man." And, in each case, it was the prophetic word that caused the man to rise up to new heights in God.

A church had lost it pastor, and the members had been looking everywhere for a suitable replacement. They had an assistant pastor, but he was so young and inexperienced that no one gave him serious consideration. When they couldn't find anyone else, however, they relented and reluctantly gave the young assistant the position of pastor.

Not long afterward God sent us to that place. We laid our hands on that young pastor and ministered to him. Before long, he was prophesying to his people and has not stopped since.

When word reached a neighboring area about what God was doing in that young pastor, he was invited to move there and take a new work. We are told that today he has several hundred young people who are on fire for God and doing a great work.

You can keep sitting at the Beautiful Gate, asking alms of the people, or you can get up in response to the word of the Lord and go *walking and leaping and praising God*. The choice is yours. Let the Spirit of God set you on your feet.

Those bones were about as hopeless as anything can get. But God is able to do whatever is necessary to get each of us up and moving for Him.

Spend time seeking God so that He will use you in the prophetic ministry.

And They Lived

What could be more impossible than believing for life for dead bones? Your situation can't be any worse than that.

Martha thought her situation was unique. When Jesus approached the tomb of Lazarus, her brother and His friend, she said:

> *Lord, by this time he stinketh: for he hath been dead four days.*   John 11:39

If you allow the natural circumstances to hinder you, you won't get anything done for God. You won't be able to speak life into anyone's life, let alone your own. If Jesus could bring Lazarus to life after four days in the grave, surely your situation is not too difficult for Him.

While ministering in Australia some years ago, I had finished my part of the service and turned the service back to the pastor. When I did, my attention was drawn to a very tall gentleman on the back seat. "Pastor," I said, "I need to pray for that man before he leaves." He called the man and his wife forward and we began to minister to them.

God spoke to them of their discouragement. He said that they had gone through times of deep trouble and trials. It had been a difficult time for them, He said. Nothing seemed to be going right. Nothing seemed to be happening. But, God said, He was now bringing them into a new time in their lives.

"Life is not finished," the Spirit said. "Indeed, new life is coming. I have something more in store for you. New doors will open to you. New opportunities to minister will be yours."

Another woman came up and joined them (we later learned that she was the mother-in-law) and God began to speak to the three of them. After the service I learned that they were preachers from New Zealand. They had been in Australia for six months, and not a single door of ministry had opened to them. They were scheduled to leave the following day because they were so discouraged. They had decided to quit the ministry and return to their secular positions. But God intervened that morning through prophecy.

A couple of years later I went to Queensland, Australia to minister. Several carloads of people met us at the airport and took us to a pastor's house. When we arrived at the house, a tall man who was opening the trunk of one of the cars said, "Brother Heflin, do you remember me? I was in your meetings years ago. I was ready to quit the ministry because of discouragement at the lack of open doors, but you prophesied to me, and my life has never been the same since then.

I am the pastor of the church where you will be ministering. From the day you prophesied to us, an excitement came into our souls, and we have had to run ever since to enter into all the doors that opened to us as a result of that night. We are enjoying working for God."

God is ready to move heaven and earth to bring to pass the things He has promised you and the things He has promised others through you. Start acting upon what God has spoken to you. Don't be afraid. And He will surely bring it to pass, FOR His promises are sure.

Lo, the Sinews Came Upon Them

When you are commanded to prophesy, you don't worry about the meaning or impact of the words you are speaking. It is because you trust God that you are speaking forth in the first place, so you trust God that He knows the why of what is being said, and you leave the results with Him. And there will be results.

What did God do for Ezekiel in the Valley of Dry Bones? He did exactly what He said He was going to do. He did exactly what Ezekiel prophesied He was going to do, because Ezekiel was just repeating what God showed him. Look closely at it:

Ezekiel said:

I will lay sinews upon you.

And what did God do?

And when I beheld, lo, the sinews ... came up upon them.

Ezekiel said:

I ... will bring up flesh upon you.

And what did God do?

And when I beheld, lo, ... the flesh came up upon them.

Ezekiel said:

I will ... cover you with skin.

And what did God do?

And when I beheld, lo, ... the skin covered them above.

Where there had been no sinew, now there was sinew. Where there had been no flesh, now there was flesh. Where there had been no skin, now there was skin. God was doing a miracle. His word was performing a creative act. Dry bones were being turned into living bodies.

Action always follows the prophetic word. Dead and hopeless things respond as the word goes forth. The devil doesn't want you to know how much power is in you. It frightens him to think that you might be let loose upon his kingdom.

If we let him, he will tie our hands and make us feel powerless. But God wants us to know that the power of the Universe has been entrusted to each of us. If you will believe and begin to act upon it, Satan will start backing up and we will see his kingdom shaken.

Therefore Prophesy

But God had not finished His work. Ezekiel was commanded to prophesy a third time.

> *Then he said unto me, Son of man, these bones are the whole house of Israel: behold, they say, Our bones are dried, and our hope is lost: we are cut off for our parts. Therefore prophesy and say unto them, Thus saith the Lord God; Behold, O my people, I will open your graves, and cause you to come up out of your graves, and bring you into the land of Israel.* Ezekiel 37:11-12

Before Ezekiel spoke, Israel was without hope. But, as we have seen, God's word brings hope into those hopeless situations. His words seemed impossible, but we have seen them come to pass.

God will do it, *therefore prophesy.*

Part III

Other Commonly Asked Questions Concerning Prophecy

Through the years, as I have made it my business to teach about the gifts of the Spirit everywhere I go, I have also developed the habit of taking time for a period of questions and answers to see what things were perplexing to the people I was ministering to and to bring them further clarification. Usually the questions are the same: Is prophecy for today? What is the purpose of it? Who can do it? When is it out of order? How can I encourage my members to start prophesying? And we have already answered those questions.

There are, however, many other questions that are expressed in these sessions, good questions, important questions, that merit some space in this volume.

Why Are Some Prophecies Not Fulfilled and Others Seem To Take So Long To Come To Pass?

It is true that some prophecies seem not to be fulfilled, while others take a long time to come to pass. Should we brand as false prophets the people who gave those prophecies? Not necessarily. Should we give up on a promise we received long ago? Definitely not! Let us look at some of the reasons prophecies are either not fulfilled or are delayed in their fulfillment.

The Matter of Timing

Everything has its proper timing, and often God speaks to us far in advance of an event to prepare us or to encourage us to work toward that goal. The actual fulfillment may take some time.

A great man of God was in my house one day in the early 80s, and I felt led to prophesy over him. One of the things God told him that day was that he would be on national television, and that it would not cost him anything. Someone else would pay the bill. He went home and told his wife that I must be one of the craziest men he had ever met. (He said it jokingly, for we are good friends.) "That man loves me so much," he told her, "that he must have prophesied out of his own spirit; for how could that ever come to pass?"

A few years went by and nothing happened. Then, one day he was invited by a major Christian network to have a regular weekly program that would be carried nationwide. There would be no cost to him, he was told. He remembered the prophecy and had to ask God to forgive him for joking about what God had said. It had happened exactly as God said it would. God had a timetable for this man getting on national television, and when that timetable was fulfilled, the prophecy came to pass.

Sometimes when we prophesy, the exact opposite of what we prophesy begins to happen. I prophesied over a pastor in Australia. He came to see me about a month later when I was in a tent meeting. He said that he had noticed that many of the prophecies I had given over members of his congregation had come to pass quickly. But with him the opposite seemed to be happening. I had prophesied several things to him: that God would fill his church, that he would have healing in his hands, and that he would be financially blessed.

He said, "You prophesied that my church would be filled, but many of my people are being moved out of the community. So many of them are moving, in fact, that it looks like I soon won't have anyone left.

"You prophesied that I would have healing in my hands, but when I pray for people to get well, they seem to get worse instead.

"And you prophesied that we would be financially blessed, but our offerings have dropped so much that if God doesn't intervene, we won't be able to finish our building.

"If anyone else had prophesied these things, I would put them down as a false prophet. But I know your life, and I don't understand what is happening to me."

I laughed. All the movement seemed to be in the wrong direction.

I said to him, "Let's try something. Don't say anything to anyone else about this. At the end of the service we will ask the pastor here to lay hands on you, and let's see what God will say through others." He agreed to the test.

At the close of the service, we were all standing together around the altar of the church. I said, "This brother needs to hear from God. Let's all open to the Lord and see what He will say."

Near the man stood a young lady, about eighteen, who had only recently started learning about prophecy. She put her hand on his shoulder and began crying and prophesying. God said through her: "I have anointed your hands, and they will be My instruments for miracles of healing. And I will fill your church. And the money you need will come in."

That pastor began laughing and weeping at the same time. We hadn't told a soul what we had discussed, but God knew all about it and had confirmed it through a young lady who only recently had begun to prophesy.

A couple of years later, I was back in Australia. In one service I was telling this story when a man in the congregation began waving his hand to speak.

"Yes, Brother," I said.

"What you are telling is true," he said. "My brother is the assistant pastor working with the man you are talking about. It happened just as the Lord had said. They finished their building, and now it is too small because God has done so many miracles of healing through the pastor that the building is always overflowing."

Part of the reason that some prophecies are delayed is that our lack of spiritual maturity limits what we can receive in God. A child may have great plans for the future, but he or she is only able to move into those plans over a period of time, a period in which they must continue to grow and to progress, to lay aside childish things and to become a mature person. Many times, God is ready to do something for us long before we are spiritually able to handle it.

Another reason for the delay may be that, in our lack of maturity, we have misunderstood entirely what God wants to do for us. As times goes on we may realize that we expected God to do one thing (because of our limited understanding) but that God has done or is doing another thing entirely. Trust Him because He knows best. He may not give you everything you want, but everything He gives you is for your personal benefit.

If a prophecy is delayed, wait patiently for it. It will be fulfilled — in God's time. If He has spoken to you in advance, it is so that you can prepare. It doesn't mean that the prophet is false.

The Matter of Satan's Opposition

While Satan is powerless to stop God's blessing on your life, he will try every measure he can to prevent your prophecy from coming to pass. It happened to Daniel:

> *But the prince of the kingdom of Persia withstood me one and twenty days: but, lo, Michael, one of the chief princes, came to help me; and I remained there with the kings of Persia.*
> Daniel 10:13

If Satan could oppose the prophet Daniel and cause a delay in the fulfillment of his promise, it can happen to you as well. He may use friends or relatives or officials or even religious leaders. But it doesn't really matter what opposition arises. If you remain firm in your trust, God will take care of you; and, in His time, the prophecy will be fulfilled.

If we will stay in the same level of anointing or grow in our spiritual lives, nothing can stop the fulfillment of the promise of God to us. Satan will use every tool at his disposal and move every person he can move to block what God intends to do for you, but he is powerless to stop it when you remain faithful. He might succeed in delaying your blessing for a short time, but that is the extent of his ability. He cannot prevent the fulfillment of the word of God.

But whatever happens, don't doubt. Hold on to the promise and contend for it, and it will be yours. The performance will surely come.

If God tells you He will save your loved ones, don't be surprised if they seem to get worse before they get better. When the devil recognizes that his time is short, he will do everything to prevent that soul from coming to God. If God said that your husband will be saved, he just might go on the biggest drunken binge he has ever been on. If God says that you son will be saved, he just might get arrested on drug charges. But whatever happens, don't lose hope. Believe God, and there will be a performance.

A gambler might get worse right before he gets better. But if God said he was going to get better, stand on that promise — no matter how bad he gets. When a sinner is at the height of conviction, he or she often reacts violently and goes to the extreme of their sin. It is not a bad sign. It is a good sign. They are miserable and will soon yield their lives to God. Keep believing. Keep trusting. Cling to the word God has given you, and look for signs of improvement.

Often sinners are not loosed from every bondage at once. Sometimes they must get one bondage broken at a time. Keep trusting. Hold on to the promise. Keep praying and believing.

When there seems to be no hope, God delights to work and to bring hope. The prophetic word creates, and the promised work will be done.

Nothing else needs to be said on this subject of Satan's opposition. Believe, and your prophetic promise will come to pass — regardless of what Satan or men or demons try to do to prevent it.

The Matter of Appropriation By Faith

If you fail to appropriate any promise as "not for me" or "not practical" or for any other reason, God is not obligated to fulfill it. Through Elizabeth, God said to Mary:

> *And blessed is she that believed: for there shall be a performance of those things which were told her from the Lord.* Luke 1:45

The performance comes only with the belief. God cannot honor your doubt. You must believe Him for His promises.

If you come to the conclusion, because of the passage of time, or because of your own failures, or for any other reason that what God said is no longer valid or was not really from God in the first place, you forfeit the promise. Every promise is received by faith.

God offers certain things to everyone in the congregation. "If you will believe me for it, your feet will soon step on foreign soil." How people react to that message will affect the outcome, and may change the course of their lives.

Some will jump to their feet and rejoice that they will soon step on foreign soil. They don't know how, but they know it will happen. And those people go — every single time.

Others will sit calmly by and wonder who will be the one to go — since their own situation would not permit it. And those people always stay behind.

The promise was for everyone, but the performance of the promise will come only to those who react favorably to God's invitation. Some don't even want to go. It would inconvenience them. So they stay behind. Others are sure they can't go. So they don't consider the message to be for them. And they, too, remain behind.

God is obligated to fulfill a promise only when we say, "Yes, that promise is for me. I receive it, and I will begin to act upon it and take every step I can to bring it to pass. Then I will leave the rest to God, and I know He will never fail."

Sometimes, when I am giving a prophecy to someone else, the promises are so wonderful that I decide to claim some of them for myself. "If God can do this thing for them," I reason, "there is no reason He can't do it for me too." And He does, even though the prophecy was primarily for another. If I believe for it, I get my share.

Many years ago, our church in Richmond was going through a great period of revival and was having all-night prayer meetings. One night, about 2 o'clock in the morning, my sister went to a young man who was seated praying, laid her hands on him and began to prophesy of revival in Ethiopia and the part God had for him to play in it. He wept, for he had long felt a great burden for Africa.

But, as often happens, he had recently gotten a new job and had bought a new car. If he left for Ethiopia at that point, he reasoned, he would probably lose his job because he hadn't been there long enough to earn that much vacation time. He would also have difficulty making the payments on his new car. So, he constantly put the matter off.

Several months went by and God began to let him know that the case was urgent. He needed to go before it was too late. My sister, Ruth, began to pray about the situation and was led to say in her prayer, "Lord, if he won't go, send me. If he won't take Your promise, I will take it for myself."

Before long, she found herself, with her companion Susan Woodaman, in Ethiopia praying in the home of a Finnish missionary. After a few days of prayer, there was a knock on the door. "Someone told us that you are praying here," the person said. "Would you mind if we joined you?" And that person was ushered in to join the prayer.

Before long, the house was full of hungry people praying for revival in Ethiopia. Before it was over, almost all of the denominational missionaries in that country had been filled with the Spirit, and great revival had broken out on the university campuses. Four or five hundred college students in Addis Ababa were filled with the Spirit and God had spoken in prophecy to the Emperor Haile Selassie about his own future and that of the nation.

God wanted to give a young man this spiritual plum, but he was not willing, so another took his place.

The Matter of Your Action of Faith

Most often, the thing that delays or prevents the fulfillment of a prophecy is our own unbelief and the lack of action of faith that results. God demands more than mental consent. He demands a demonstration of your faith, and that demonstration requires some action on your part.

If the Lord tells you that this will be the greatest year you have ever had, get ready for the greatest year you have ever had. Satan will try to stop it, but he is powerless to do it. It will come — as you believe God for it.

One New Years Eve God spoke to us that we were on the brink of something new and great. I got busy calling nationally prominent ministers to come and speak for us at our campmeeting that year. I submitted immediately to the County Planning Commission a plan to enlarge our outdoor Tabernacle, and we prepared ads to run in the largest circulation Christian magazine in America. When God speaks, He knows what He is doing, and we must respond favorably.

God told Noah it was going to rain, so he began building an ark. God told Joshua he was going to be victorious in battle the following day, so he told the people to prepare. God told Moses that tomorrow would be the day for leaving Egypt, so he told the children of Israel to be packed and to keep their shoes and clothes on all night so they could leave early in the morning.

When God speaks, don't just sit back waiting to see if something will happen. Start acting on what God has spoken, and it will come to pass.

If God tells you that He will fill your church, start looking for a bigger place. It doesn't matter what the present reality is. If God tells you He is going to do something, He will do it.

When God tells you that you will travel for Him, go home and get a suitcase out and start packing a few things. Get your travel documents in order. Set your personal affairs in order so that you can be absent for a time without causing serious disruption in the family. Act on what God is saying. Pack a towel and wash cloth. Pack some toothpaste, some shaving cream or some hair spray. Take a step of faith.

When God speaks of revival, get ready for revival. Most of us wouldn't know what to do with revival if it came to us. Most churches wouldn't be ready to receive large numbers of people if they did get saved. If we don't believe what God is saying, we won't act on it, therefore God can't do what He promised because we are not ready to receive it and because we have not demonstrated faith in His word. Do something. Demonstrate your faith.

How can God send great numbers of new believers to your church if you don't have prepared teachers who will care for those new believers? You have to get ready.

How can God double the size of a congregation if there is no physical room to put them in the building? You have to get ready. How can God send you to the nations if you have no passport? You have to get ready. How can God use you to heal people if you never lay your hands on any sick? How can God use you to win the lost if you never go to them?

In 1965 I received a prophecy from my mother. I had just returned from great revivals, and among other things God said to me, "Miracles do happen — when you fast and when you pray." I have never forgotten that word, and when I am out in special meetings anywhere in the world, I remind the Lord of what He said. Then I act by faith. I start fasting and praying. When I do, I expect to see the results, and they always come.

The reason your action of faith is so important is that every prophetic promise is conditional. God says to us, "If you will do this, I will do that." Therefore, the fulfillment of His promise largely depends on us. God will not fail us — if we are obedient to our part of the bargain. If we meet God's conditions, He never fails us.

When we stop walking with God and doing His will, however, His blessings stop flowing. That doesn't mean that God failed. It usually means that we failed.

The fact that God requires your action of faith doesn't mean that He needs your help. It just means that He has set some simple task for you as a test of your love and obedience to Him, and when you have obeyed in that simple task, it shows Him your seriousness.

When Abraham took Isaac up to Mt. Moriah, prepared an altar, prepared the wood for a fire to make a sacrifice, and had his hand raised to take the life of his son, God said to him:

> *Lay not thine hand upon the lad, neither do thou any thing unto him: for now I know that thou fearest God, seeing thou hast not withheld thy son, thine only son from me.* Genesis 22:12

Thank God that we are not called upon to make the same sacrifices Abraham faced. He was to be the father of our faith and, as such, had to face the most severe trials. The things God asks us to do pale by comparison. They are simple acts of faith, simple acts of obedience, simple demonstrations of love. That's all God requires of us.

It Works

In 1966, Sister Gwen Shaw, the founder of End Time Handmaidens of Arkansas, prophesied over me. Through her, God said to me, "You will preach from the Near East to the Far East and from Australia to the Northlands." I kept a typed copy of that prophecy in my Bible and, from the summer of 1966 until January of 1981, I tried to discover what God meant by "the Northlands." During that time, I did preach from the Near East to the Far East, and I went to Australia a number of times; but I could not discover what God meant by "the Northlands." No one I asked had ever heard of it.

Since it was connected to Australia in the prophecy, I thought it surely had something to do with that county. So I asked many Australians, "Where are the Northlands?" But none of them seemed to know.

"We have the Northshore," they said.

"Would it be in New Zealand?" I asked a few New Zealanders I met.

"I don't think so," they replied. "We have the North Island, but not the Northlands."

I decided that "the Northlands" must be in Finland, in what is known as Lapland. That made sense to me because that area lies so far north. But nobody in Finland seemed to know anything about "the Northlands."

Many years passed. When I went forward to give an offering in the camp in 1980, my uncle, Dr. William A. Ward, laid hands on me and prophesied that I would visit New Zealand and Australia. I had, by that time, been to Australia ten times, but I was excited about the prospect of preaching in New Zealand for the very first time.

One day that winter I felt that it would soon be time to go on this journey, so I called a brother I knew in New Zealand and told him that I would be arriving there two weeks later. He used that two weeks to arrange my itinerary. I left home in the middle of winter and arrived in New Zealand during the height of their summer. And, oh was it hot!

The brother was late arriving at the airport, so when he did arrive we had only a few minutes in which he could hand me a stack of airline tickets and a schedule he had worked out for me with local pastors, and I had to run to catch my next flight.

I wasn't able to look over the schedule until the plane took off. When I did, I saw some of the strangest names I had ever heard anywhere in the world: Hickorangi, Pickawhoi, and many other of those Maori names. I had no idea what was in store for me in those exotic places, but as I thought on them I was reminded of the prophecy concerning "the Northlands."

A preacher was waiting for me at the end of my flight. When we were sitting in his car, I asked him the question I had asked so many other people before him: "Do you know anything about the North-lands"?

He laughed. "Your entire itinerary is in the Northlands," he said. And I will never forget the out-pouring of the Spirit that followed in the Northlands. As I was to learn, the Northlands was where Captain Cook landed in New Zealand, where the first Euro-pean settlements were made, and where the first school and the first church were established in that country. It was in the Northlands that missionaries first established an outstation in New Zealand.

It had taken me fifteen years to find it, but I found it. Don't give up on God's promises. Cling to them. He never fails.

The fact that it took me fifteen years to get to the Northlands of New Zealand did not make Sister Gwen Shaw a false prophet. She had spoken the truth. For whatever reason, it took me a long time to see the fulfillment. But I got there. That is the impor-tant thing.

Many of the prophecies of the Old Testament were fulfilled only in a limited sense during the lifetime of the prophet. They were for a future generation. It took some eight hundred years for the prophecies of Isaiah about the birth of Jesus to come to pass. But they did come to pass — in every detail. So don't brand the prophet false just because a prophecy is delayed in its fulfillment.

But also don't expect to wait hundreds of years for the fulfillment of your prophetic promises. We are not living in such an ancient time and most of our prophecies could not take so long to be fulfilled. Be patient, and trust the Lord, and He will bring it to pass everything that He has promised.

God said through Habakkuk:

> *For the vision is yet for an appointed time, but at the end it shall speak, and not lie: though it tarry, wait for it; because it will surely come, it will not tarry.* Habakkuk 2:3

That promise almost seems like a contradiction: *"Though it tarry, ... it will not tarry."* What God is saying is that He is never late. He knows the timing of all things. And He moves in the proper time. When God seems to be late in working for you, don't despair, for His timing is perfect.

Each of us has received prophetic promises that have not yet been fulfilled. And there may be a variety of reasons that they have not been fulfilled: the timing of God, our own lack of maturity, lack of obedience or lack of faith. But God has not finished with us yet. Hold on to every promise.

God has not forgotten, and you must not forget either. The fact that time has passed, even much time, does not make the person who prophesied a false prophet. Hold on to your prophetic promise.

Occasionally, when I feel that I have done everything I know to do to receive a promise God has given me and it still doesn't come, I just leave it with God. In His time and in His way, He will bring it to pass. He never fails and His word never fails.

- 10 -

Is Prophecy Always Positive?

The proper content of prophecy, especially personal prophecy, is often questioned. Is it proper to use prophecy for rebuke? Is prophecy always positive?

Edification, Exhortation and Comfort

As a general rule, all prophecy is positive. Paul declared prophecy to be for *"edification, exhortation and comfort,"* and those are all positive elements.

God's great love for His people compels Him to always speak words of encouragement. He doesn't look at what we now are but at what we can become in Him. He doesn't look at our present limitations but at our huge potential. He doesn't look at our present lack but knows the bounty of goodness He has stored up for us. And He can find something good to say to the worst of individuals because He foresees something good in store for them — as they will obey His voice.

When many people think of prophecy, they picture an Old Testament prophet calling down judgment upon an individual, a city or a nation. And some delight in this type of harsh utterance. But New Testament prophecy is decidedly different in this regard.

When the disciples suggested that they call fire down from heaven to consume some who were not in agreement with them (as, they said, Elijah had done), Jesus rebuked them:

> *And when his disciples James and John saw this, they said, Lord, wilt thou that we command fire to come down from heaven, and consume them, even as Elias did? But he turned, and rebuked them, and said, Ye know not what manner of spirit ye are of. For the Son of man is not come to destroy men's lives, but to save them. And they went to another village.* Luke 9:54-56

The New Testament is clear:

> *I am not come to destroy, but to fulfil.* Matthew 5:17

> *For God sent not his Son into the world to condemn the world; but that the world through him might be saved.* John 3:17

The Scriptures say of *all the promises of God* that they are *yea* and *amen*.

> *For all the promises of God in him are yea, and*
> *in him Amen, unto the glory of God by us.*
> 2 Corinthians 1:20

This includes prophetic promises as well as the promises of the written Word. *All* the promises of God are *yea*. *All* the promises of God are *amen*. That is positive. That is encouraging. Therefore, any prophecy that is harsh, uncaring, and personally offensive, cannot be from God. But ...

There is a "but." Some of us are offended by God's caring words of love. Some of us are offended when He wants to touch areas of our lives that need His attention, and we have declared those areas off limits to His intervention. Some of us are so self-willed that we are offended by the knowledge of what God wants for our lives.

So, there is a BUT. And that BUT is that God has the right to speak to us what He knows to be good for us — whether we like it or not.

Is Rebuke Positive?

Some of us would consider rebuke to be uncaring, harsh and offensive. But God said He does it because He loves us:

> *And ye have forgotten the exhortation which*
> *speaketh unto you as unto children, My son,*
> *despise not thou the chastening of the Lord, nor*

*faint when thou art rebuked of him: For whom
the Lord loveth he chasteneth, and scourgeth every son whom he receiveth. If ye endure
chastening, God dealeth with you as with sons;
for what son is he whom the father chasteneth
not? But if ye be without chastisement, whereof
all are partakers, then are ye bastards, and not
sons.*   Hebrews 12:5-8

*But when we are judged, we are chastened of the
Lord, that we should not be condemned with the
world.*   1 Corinthians 11:32

The purpose of God's setting the ministries in the
Church is *for the perfecting of the saints,* and that includes prophecy. But in order to bring about the
spiritual perfection or maturity that He desires for
us, He has to deal with anything in us which is imperfect or immature. That hurts, but it has to be done.

If everyone continually pats us on the back and
tells us how well we are doing, and no one has the
courage to point out how we can do better, we become spiritual cripples, locked into some weakness
of the flesh. In order to make us strong, God has to
deal with our weaknesses. Let Him do that without
resentment.

If God doesn't point out the ruts we are in, how can
we get out of them? If He doesn't show us a better
way to do things, how can we know it exists? Don't
resent His words of love.

Nothing that God says is said with a spirit of vindictiveness. Nothing that He says is said with envy or vainglory or strife. Everything that He says emanates from His heart of love for you.

When God called Jeremiah to be a prophet, He said to him:

> *See, I have this day set thee over the nations and over the kingdoms, to root out, and to pull down, and to destroy, and to throw down, to build, and to plant.*   Jeremiah 1:10

We all want to *build* and to *plant,* but in order to *build* and to *plant*, it is sometimes necessary to *root out*, to *pull down* and to *destroy* first.

Exhortation often seems harsh, as when a father speaks heart to heart with his son. But our heavenly Father has every right to correct us, and if He doesn't do it we should think it strange. If you need it, welcome it.

God does all of this in a very positive way. When He wants to tell someone that they are stubborn and other people are listening, He has a very gentle way of doing it. He may speak concerning "the dangers of following your own will," or that "you have not always followed My will as closely as you should." He may even disguise completely what He is saying so that only the person hearing understands completely. He will never do anything to embarrass you. He loves you.

Expect Some Resentment

Some people resent prophecy that goes beyond the surface of their lives, and they will resent you for giving such a prophecy. They would rather remain in their comfortable situation and don't want you stirring up their nest. They don't want you challenging them to new and better things. They don't want to hear that God's will for them is higher and greater than they are presently experiencing.

As a result, you will get some persecution when you speak God's mind. Just be sure you are doing the right thing, and don't worry about how people might react to it. They are not rejecting you, but they are rejecting God and His will for their lives. There is no rule to say that everyone will love you for speaking the truth.

For instance, God spoke to a young lady in the southern part of America, a young lady that everyone recognized as a potential missionary. He said, "Don't spend all your time doing your own thing and neglect to spend time with Me in prayer." She resented that word, and it was easy to see her resentment. Later, she tried to convince everyone that the message had really been for someone else. She couldn't stand the thought that she wasn't as spiritual as she ought to be.

Many of us don't like it when God deals with our flesh. We want to think we are already the best. Let's not attack the messenger just because God has something important to say to us. If we had seen that truth ourselves, perhaps we wouldn't have needed someone else to point it out to us.

The easy thing would be to always skim the surface and to never deal with difficult issues in prophecy. It is easy to always speak honeyed words. But it takes far more boldness and maturity to speak forth the hurtful things that many need to hear. It takes a real man or woman of maturity to deal with the delicate matters. You can choose to avoid conflict and resentment and stay in the shallows, or you can decide to allow God to use you in a greater depth of prophecy, and dedicate yourself to personal maturity so that He can trust you with the riches of His grace.

I understand why some people react badly to prophecy. It doesn't necessarily mean that they are bad people. I haven't always appreciated every word I received through the years, at the moment it was spoken. But, as I considered it, I realized that God only wanted to be sure that I was used to my full potential. And as I gratefully accepted His word, He did the work in me. Be patient with immature believers and help them go on to greater things in God.

Prophecy is always positive, but be sure you appreciate every positive message from God.

- 11 -

What Does the Bible Mean By the Phrase *"Let the Other Judge"*?

In writing to the Corinthian Church, Paul stated:

> *Let the prophets speak two or three, and let the other judge.*   1 Corinthians 14:29

Many have interpreted this passage to mean that wrong things are said in prophecy and that we must divide the good from the bad and decide for ourselves what to accept. Some churches even have judges that are assigned to do this work.

Some churches have come out with the teaching that prophecy should be submitted with anticipation in writing to the leadership of the church so that they can judge it and decide if it is for the entire congregation. That is against the nature of true prophecy. It does not come "with anticipation." It is spontaneous. It is not planned. It is not something we meditate upon before hand.

I cannot accept the interpretation of this passage as meaning that we must pick and choose what we accept from a given prophecy, for it does nothing but spread fear and uncertainty. If some of what is said in prophecy is not acceptable, how can I be sure what portion to trust? I'm not smart enough to make that decision. I might reject only the part I didn't understand or the part I didn't agree with or the part I really didn't want to hear. So that simply cannot be the case.

When we *judge*, therefore, we are judging the prophet not the prophecy. The Bible says:

> *Beloved, believe not every spirit, but try the spirits whether they are of God: because many false prophets are gone out into the world.*
> 1 John 4:1

And we are given, by Jesus, ways of identifying false prophets.

> *Beware of false prophets, which come to you in sheep's clothing, but inwardly they are ravening wolves. Ye shall know them by their fruits. Do men gather grapes of thorns, or figs of thistles? Even so every good tree bringeth forth good fruit; but a corrupt tree bringeth forth evil fruit. A good tree cannot bring forth evil fruit, neither can a corrupt tree bring forth good fruit. Every tree that bringeth not forth good fruit is hewn*

> *down, and cast into the fire. Wherefore by their*
> *fruits ye shall know them.*   Matthew 7:15-20

Because I never want to have to be judgmental about a word given to me, I am careful about who prays over me. That way I don't have to be critical and sort out every word in judgment.

If you are living a loose life, if you are up and down and in and out of the life of the Spirit, please don't lay your hand on me and prophesy. I don't want to receive of your carnality.

On the other hand, we cannot expect to be perfect before God begins to use us in the gifts of the Spirit. I will gladly let anyone who is dedicated to God and faithful to His Word and His house to lay hands on me and prophesy. I am that sure of what God does.

Judging, then, in the sense that many use the word, is very dangerous. It is too easy to dismiss something that you don't understand as being "of the flesh" or "not of God." It is too easy to dismiss something that makes you uncomfortable as being "of the flesh" or "not of God." It is too easy to dismiss something that you don't want to obey as being "of the flesh" or "not of God."

Don't dismiss immediately everything you don't understand or everything that makes you feel uncomfortable. If you do, God can't do anything new for you. He can't stretch you out of your comfort zone into new things in Him.

We simply cannot pick apart every word given to us in prophecy or we will be choosing what we like and not what is good for us. It would be like letting children choose what they will eat. They will choose ice cream and candy and whipped cream every time. And only rarely will they choose potatoes and beans and meat, the very things they need.

When I find a person who fears God and is living a life of example, I am open to what they have to say to me. I don't choose what I want to believe and what I don't want to believe.

When I know, on the other hand, that a person is not right in their spirit, I don't trust anything they say. I don't want them laying hands on me, and I won't receive their prophecy. This way I avoid false prophets.

Paul, in writing to the Corinthians, gave them one basic rule in regard to false prophets.

> *Wherefore I give you to understand, that no man speaking by the Spirit of God calleth Jesus accursed: and that no man can say that Jesus is the Lord, but by the Holy Ghost.*
> 1 Corinthians 12:3

Another basic rule is that prophecy can never contradict the Bible.

But most false prophets are very subtle. They use the Scriptures and use the name of Jesus freely. There are only two ways to know them: (1) in the Spirit and (2) by their fruits. Know them and avoid them.

But don't judge individual prophecies. Rather than everyone sitting around with our arms crossed trying to decide whether a prophecy is "of God" or not, we need more wise people in the Church like both Joseph and Daniel who became interpreters of dreams and of "hard sayings." They brought clarification to the things God was saying in their day. It is not uncommon for those who are hearing from God to misinterpret what He is saying. He means one things and we understand something else. Where are the Daniels and Josephs of our time? They represent the wise judges needed in the Church today.

- 12 -

Other Questions Concerning Prophecy

Is It Biblical to Prophesy to Yourself?

Prophesying to yourself, in the general sense of the phrase, doesn't make sense. If you can hear God's voice, why do you need to speak it out to yourself? You already know what you are going to say before you say it. So why say it? In the same way, it is not necessary to speak in tongues and then give yourself the interpretation. If God can speak to you directly, you have already heard from God. Why speak it forth to yourself? It has no purpose.

As we have noted, it is effective at times to prophesy to your situation, to your pocketbook, to your health, to your family, to your job situation. But should we be prophesying to ourselves?

If you are living close enough to God to hear His voice for yourself and you receive a word from Him, you already have that word. What would be gained by prophesying it to yourself? Just receive it in your spirit. If you can receive an interpretation of a message in tongues, you already have the message. What is gained by speaking it out to yourself?

This may seem necessary to those who are childish in their spiritual walk. But surely we should go on to other things.

Most people would never think of prophesying to themselves in the midst of the congregation. It wouldn't make sense. Then why would they think of it at home? Some people who believe they have only one of the inspiration gifts, tongues, interpretation, or prophecy, do this. They are wrong. We can all hear the voice of God. We can all know His will. We can all receive His guidance.

Prophesy to your situation. Prophesy to your enemies. Prophesy to your sickness. Prophesy to your pocketbook. But there is no need to prophesy to yourself.

The gifts of the Spirit, in general, are for the edification of the Body of Christ. They are a means of sharing with the entire body our personal revelations. If you already have the revelation, why do you need to prophesy it to yourself?

What Did God Mean By *"Do My Prophets No Harm"*?

He suffered no man to do them wrong: yea, he reproved kings for their sakes, Saying, Touch not mine anointed, and do my prophets no harm.
                                            1 Chronicles 16:21-22

This command dates from antiquity. God spoke it before His people came into the land of Canaan, while Abraham was still passing from nation to nation on his way to the promised land. It was a warning from God to the nations. They must not harm His prophets.

The command was later repeated almost word for word in the Psalms:

> *He suffered no man to do them wrong: yea, he*
> *reproved kings for their sakes; Saying, Touch*
> *not mine anointed, and do my prophets no harm.*
>   Psalms 105:14-15

God reproved kings in this matter. He warned all nations. We must not despise a prophet of God. When we reject a true prophet of God, we are rejecting God Himself. And when we reject out of hand the words of a true prophet of God, we are rejecting out of hand the words of God Himself.

What Is the Relationship Between Prophecy and the Other Gifts of the Spirit and Between the Office of the Prophet and Other Ministries?

The gifts of the Spirit work together like bacon and eggs, or salt and pepper. They are companions. And several gifts are usually needed to minister to a person in need. Let me give you a hypothetical example:

Let's say I am called in the middle of the night to go pray for a lady who is dying. On the way to the hospital, I am praying about how I will deal with this situation, and God shows me that the woman is sick because she has bitterness in her heart against another sister. I become convinced that if the woman will confess her bitterness, God will rid her of it and also heal her body. So, in a moment's time, I have received a word of knowledge about what is wrong and a word of wisdom concerning what to do about it.

When I arrive at the hospital, I say to the sister, "God has shown me that you have something in your heart against your sister. If you will ask Him to forgive you, He will forgive you and will also heal you."

As I lay hands on the woman, I feel supernatural faith coming to me and I declare the words of healing. The gift of healing begins to work, and within minutes the woman is rejoicing in her new-found liberty, both spiritual and physical. I have exercised at least four of the gifts of the Spirit in ministering to her need.

The prophetic word that goes forth may be mixed with the word of knowledge, the word of wisdom, the discerning of spirits, the gift of faith, the working of miracles and the gifts of healing. Sometimes five or six gifts can be at work at one time. A prophet needs many gifts to operate successfully.

The ministries also overlap in this same way. The fact that Jeremiah was called to be a prophet did not mean that he did not have a pastor's heart or have the burden of an evangelist or of a teacher. His special calling was to be a prophet, but he had elements of many other ministries at work in his life.

Those who are called to be pastors can go out and evangelize. And evangelists can teach when they need to. Although each of us has a particular calling, as servants of God, we must demonstrate our love though many areas of ministry.

I am an evangelist and have had to pray for a pastor's heart to maintain the church God and our parents entrusted to us. But there is entirely too much emphasis on particular ministries today. Some people worry themselves to death trying to discover what exactly they are in the Body of Christ.

There is nothing wrong with discovering your particular area of calling and of preparing yourself to the best of your ability to perform that calling, but let God use you in the area of ministry He needs you in today.

My father had an apostle's heart. When he drove through a town, he was not looking at the beautiful parks or the fine real estate. He was looking for a lot where he could erect his tent and a storefront building where he could start a new church. That was his burden. He was a church planter. Yet he was also a pastor and a teacher and an evangelist. Let God give you a well-rounded ministry.

Is There A Difference Between Exercising the Gift of Prophecy and Being A Prophet?

Yes, there is a difference. Although all may prophesy, that is everyone may exercise the gift of prophecy, it is something very different to be called to the office of a prophet. A person who dedicates himself to seeking God in fasting and prayer and living a holy life before the Lord may be called into a position of ministry that is far different than just giving an occasional prophecy.

Being a prophet requires of us a much deeper commitment to God and to His work. It is certainly a full time job and a serious one.

I would caution those who are called to this office to guard themselves in a special way against pride. In particular, let me say that it is always better not to put a title on yourself, to say that you are a prophet. Let the gift speak for itself. There are too many who have labeled themselves "prophet" when they didn't have the fruit or gifts to back up such a title. The title is often used in pride, and that is a dangerous thing.

I personally don't think it is proper for anyone to place the title "Prophet" on their calling card. I feel the same way about the title "Apostle." Let your works speak for you. And if you are worthy of praise, let another praise you. Don't praise yourself. There have been too many abuses in the past in this regard.

What Does God Mean By
"Diversity of Gifts"?

In that marvelous twelfth chapter of 1 Corinthians, Paul wrote:

> *Now there are DIVERSITIES of gifts, but the same Spirit. And there are DIFFERENCES of administrations, but the same Lord. And there are DIVERSITIES of operations, but it is the same God which worketh all in all.*
>
> 1 Corinthians 12:4-6

What does it mean to have *diversities of gifts, differences of administrations* and *diversities of operations*? It just means they are different. There are nine different gifts and there are differences in how those nine gifts are manifested in various individuals.

Just because a gift is operated differently doesn't make it wrong. God has placed great diversity in the Body in this regard. The same Spirit moves through different individuals in different ways, producing *diversities of gifts.*

You don't have to do it like I do it; and I don't have to do it like you do it. I am a unique individual and you are another unique individual. What each of us needs to do is to become sensitive to the moving of the Spirit and be obedient to His voice.

This is the beauty of a choir. We take many unique voices, each of them beautiful in their own way, and through the use of a choir director that everyone follows make those many voices blend into one great voice. This is what God wants for His Body, for all the various parts to work together for the benefit of the whole.

There are many ways to operate the word of knowledge, for example. And, in the same way, there are many ways to operate the gift of prophecy. We cannot establish a set pattern and put the same stamp on each believer. God has made each of us unique, as it pleases Him.

God will take the uniqueness of each of us, what others might call our peculiarities, and use them for His glory. Let Him work as He desires to work. Don't limit the Spirit of God. He has many wonderful things in store that we have never yet dreamed of.

Perhaps I will not operate tomorrow in the Spirit as I do today. The Spirit has control of that, and He has chosen to place *diversity* in the Body.

As you grow in God, expect Him to deal with you in an altogether different way. He is a God of diversity and you cannot expect Him to do things the same way every time. As you grow spiritually, He will change the way He deals with you and will give you a new variety of experience.

What Is the Difference Between Prophecy and the Gift of Tongues With Interpretation?

Both the purpose and the result of the gifts of tongues with interpretation and prophecy are the same. So, prophecy is greater only in the sense that it is done in half the time and with half the energy.

But it takes greater faith to prophesy than it does to speak in tongues. One reason is that no one understands you when you speak in tongues, so they can't criticize you as easily. When you prophesy, everyone understands the words you are saying.

Tongues serves, the Scriptures teach us, as a *sign to the unbeliever*. And when all of those present are believers, it is God's perfect plan to use prophecy instead. If we are sufficiently mature in the Spirit, we can omit the speaking in tongues and go directly into prophecy. However, because we are all in different stages of spiritual growth and maturity, there will always be messages in tongues in our services.

Paul taught:

> *If any man speak in an unknown tongue, let it be by two, or at the most by three, and that by course; and let one interpret.*
> 1 Corinthians 14:27

The only thing God is saying here is that if you get a long message in tongues it is difficult to digest it all at once. This is the reason the exercise of the gifts of the Spirit are to be *by course*.

Some churches cut off the Holy Spirit when there have been three messages in tongues with interpretations in a service. Many times, however, when there are several messages in tongues with interpretation, one after the other, the second is a continuation of the first, and the third is a continuation of the second. The Holy Spirit breaks up the message into shorter segments so that we can digest it properly. And since, this is technically one message, another message may be given later in the service.

In a large Chinese meal, the food is served in courses. The courses are varied so that you don't get tired of one thing. When you eat slowly, conversing with those around you, the meal can go on for an extended period and you can consume an amazing amount of food. You couldn't eat that much if you tried to do it all at once or if you tried to eat that same amount of one dish. By varying the dishes and bringing them a little at a time, you find yourself eating much more than you would have otherwise. That is what God wants in the church.

If all that food were brought at the very first and placed before you, you would be repulsed by it. It would seem impossible to eat. Yet, presenting it in this way changes everything, and you go away feeling that the Chinese feast was a wonderful experience that you would like to repeat often.

The case of having too many messages in tongues is not a common one in the world today. If you encounter this problem, however, there is a simple solution. Encourage those who are speaking in tongues and interpretation to take a further step in God and move into prophecy and since God said, *'Ye may all prophesy,'* the problem will be eliminated.

Who Are the Two Witnesses
of the Book of Revelation?

The two witnesses of the Book of Revelation are two prophets who will prophesy in the streets of Jerusalem for three years. The attention of the whole world will be drawn to these two men, who will become a thorn in the side of unbelieving men. These will be God's representatives of the moment, just as we are in our time.

> *And I will give power unto my two witnesses, and they shall prophesy a thousand two hundred and threescore days, clothed in sackcloth.*
> Revelation 11:3

> *And when they shall have finished their testimony, the beast that ascendeth out of the bottomless pit shall make war against them, and shall overcome them, and kill them.*
> Revelation 11:7

Part IV

Going Deeper In Prophecy

- 13 -

The Seven Depths of Prophecy

I was in California many years ago, preaching for a lady pastor that I consider to be one of the greatest prophetesses I have ever known. She was one of those who helped to pray me through to salvation and the Holy Ghost in Seattle, Washington. She often had people call her from many parts of the world and, without knowing anything at all about them, she would begin to prophesy to them in detail over the phone. And her prophecies came to pass to the letter.

Because of her unusual gift, two tape recorders were kept running constantly in her services so as not to miss anything that God was saying. Her Sunday morning service would often continue late into the afternoon.

One day while I was there she said to me, "Are you aware that there are at least seven depths of prophecy?" I wasn't aware of any such thing. I thought prophecy was prophecy, and her comment shocked me.

"Her Comment Shocked Me!"

She explained that there was *general prophecy*, which usually applies to anybody, and therefore cannot be very specific or detailed.

Congregational prophecy may also be quite general, but must deal with some of the specific needs and goals of the local congregation.

Area prophecy, in the same way, may have generalized parts, but deals with the specific needs and goals of a geographic area.

National prophecy, because it relates to many people, will be generalized, but must be specific to the nation to which it is directed.

International prophecy must apply to a broad spectrum of people, but also deals with specific world events, specific times, and specific places.

Personal prophecy, because it *is* personal, has the potential of being the most specific and detailed of all the depths of prophecy.

But *directional prophecy* is probably the deepest form of prophecy. It is so important to the life of an individual, a congregation or a nation, that it must be clear and concise and understandable. Many people's futures depend on it.

Each of these levels of prophecy is deeper than the other and therefore demands of us a deeper consecration to God to exercise effectively. It is clearly one thing to prophesy, "Many natural disasters will come to America in the days ahead," and to prophesy, "Tomorrow, about this time, a certain specific city, in a certain specific state, will be hit by a strong wind storm."

It is one thing to prophesy over someone that they will make a missionary journey, but it is quite another thing to give them specific details about what to expect, what to avoid, and where to go and not go.

At some point our prophecies must become more detailed than, "Thus saith the Lord, 'I want to bless you.' " It is the detail we speak forth that lets men and women know that God is speaking through us. When we say things that no one else knows, there is no other explanation for it, and the hearts of the people are convinced. And the more detailed our prophecies become the more valuable they are to those who hear us. The longer we wait upon the Lord the more detail He can give us. And, as we grow in God and in our intimate relationship with Him, greater things will be revealed to us and greater things will be spoken through us.

Since each of the levels of prophecy demands a greater accuracy and detail, it also takes another step of faith on the part of the prophet to speak forth such prophecy. It is not necessarily more difficult, and anyone who is willing to open to God can do it. It just requires a new step out into the unknown realm. But God knows what will happen tomorrow, and He can tell you all about it, if you are listening.

After my pastor friend told me about the seven levels of prophecy, I was thinking more about it on the plane going back home to Virginia. If there are at least seven depths of prophecy, I realized, there must be at least seven depths of the others gifts as well. And since there are nine gifts, and at least seven depths of each, that means there are at least sixty-three different experiences awaiting each of us, just in the operation of the gifts of the Spirit. Yet, some of us get our toes wet in the Spirit, and we shout, "I've got it. I've got it," and are satisfied.

There are many other levels of anointing and many other levels of revelation that may accompany each of the gifts, so we are only beginning to touch the glory that God has prepared for each of us. Don't be satisfied with a drop when God has prepared an oceanful.

The important thing for each of us is not to become stagnated in our Christian experience, but to press on constantly into new realms of the Spirit, to press on constantly into new depths of His glory. Let us allow more variety to come into our lives. There are depths of prophecy that none of us have yet experienced. We are only getting started.

Those who don't believe in prophecy are the losers. How they have come to their wrong conclusions, I can't imagine. They may have had some bad experiences that led them to believe as they do. May you and I live a life of which the devil cannot take advantage in this way.

Prepare To Be Used

As a minister of the Gospel, I have a responsibility to my people to stay in the place of close intimacy with God so that He can work through me to meet their needs. I feel this responsibility more and more as the time of the end approaches. And I constantly present myself before God as a prime candidate for His movement in my life. I am ready to do things that may seem foolish or even ridiculous to others, if that is what will bring glory to God and build His kingdom in the hearts of men.

I am determined to avoid things that would bind me and make me ineligible for this work. I want to stay free so that God can use me in this special way. And I urge you not to let anything in your life distract from the task ahead. Let nothing hinder the anointing you are wearing. And let your life support what you are proclaiming in the Spirit.

You must prepare for great things. If God called Jeremiah to be a prophet to the nations, why not you? God had a plan for Jeremiah even before he was formed in his mother's womb, and He has a plan for your life and for mine. He hears the cry of the discouraged people in this world, and His heart is moved to send someone to reach them. Will you answer the call?

Don't wait on a great man or woman to come along. The time has passed when God would use only a few chosen people. This is a different age. He is picking up unknown and unheralded individuals and using them for His glory.

God is raising up obscure people, those we would call "nobodies." But there are no *nobodies* in God's Kingdom. We all have an important role to play in His plan. He is calling His people from the back side of the desert, from alongside the Brook Cherith and from Egypt, and is using all those who will hear His voice.

You may not have anything that sets you apart physically, but when God begins to work through you, people will take notice. God is moving in new ways. Get into His move.

Get ready to work hard because there is a great harvest out there waiting to be reaped. Get ready to work hard because God is looking for laborers.

If you are not using the abilities God has already given you, don't be expecting Him to give you more. And if your God-given abilities remain unused, even those you have will diminish. But if you use what God has given you, there is no limit to what He will do through you.

Learn From Your Mistakes

Learn from your mistakes and don't repeat them. None of us lives up to the high standards that God has set for us. But that doesn't mean that we stop trying. We are ever-striving for greater holiness and greater anointing and greater insight into His will, and thus, we should be continually moving into greater fulfillment of His promises.

One of the mistakes that those who are just beginning often make is to feel that since another has more experience, those who are less experienced should keep quiet and let others prophesy. If that is true, how will you ever learn? Yes, there may be those who are more experienced, but you have to grow in your experience too. There is a time to honor another, and there is a time for you to speak, although an honored one may be present.

The only way you can learn swimming is by swimming. If you sit on the side of the pool because there are other, more experienced, swimmers present, you will never learn; and when those better swimmers go somewhere else, there will be no one to replace them. Get out into the water and start swimming.

Some say they are afraid to prophesy because they are afraid to be an embarrassment to God. If you feel that way, you are already an embarrassment to God — because you think you are wiser than He is and can run the House of God better than He can. If you are one of those who are afraid to prophesy for fear of being in the flesh, you are already in the flesh. And you will remain in the flesh, as long as you resist obedience to God.

Learn from your mistakes. Don't let them drag you down into uselessness.

Reject All Fear

Since God uses us according to the level of our faith, the Spirit is challenging us to take greater steps of faith so that we can be more mightily used. And taking steps of faith requires that we reject all fear.

When any fear comes to you concerning the gifts of the Spirit, you can know that it does not come from God. Fear is of the devil. The devil doesn't want you to prophesy. He doesn't want you to bless people. He doesn't want you to bring deliverance to captives. He doesn't want you to help people know the will of God for their lives.

So of course he will try to make you afraid. But forge ahead — without fear. Reject his every insinuation and cling to the promise of God.

If you give someone a prophecy and you are not satisfied with the result, don't get upset about it. Believe God for a second opportunity to put your hands on them and give a further insight into God's will for their lives. Believe God for a greater anointing so that your words will have a greater impact upon their lives the next time.

The simplicity that is necessary to believe God's simple promises and to move out into prophetic ministry might be termed foolishness by some. That's okay. Let them think what they will. We will just keep enjoying the blessings of God.

Don't Run From Change

If you are afraid of change, don't become a prophet of God, because prophecy brings change. If you don't want to shake things up everywhere you go, then don't become a prophet because prophecy brings change. If you don't want to be blamed for turning things upside down, then don't become a prophet of God because prophecy brings change.

Some people are satisfied and don't want their life to be disturbed. They are not candidates for prophecy because prophecy brings change.

Those dead bones were nothing but dead bones. But when the prophetic word was spoken, the dead bones became bones with sinews. Then they became bones with sinews and flesh. Then they became bones with sinews, flesh and skin. And finally they stood up and became a great army. The prophetic word is creative and powerful. It can make things that are from things that are not.

We may not be able to see what is happening, but the word will be working until change comes, just as surely as God brought light out of darkness by His Word. There are no limits of time or space on God's word.

The end times are upon us, and God needs an army in these closing days of the twentieth century. If you are willing to become His recruit, let us go forth together and raise up some dry bones to become soldiers in that great army. God is stirring up gifts in His people and causing us to be part of what He is doing.

If you have begun to move into the things of God, don't stop now. This is only the beginning of many wonderful things in Him. There are many levels of anointing in God, many levels of prophecy, and many other exciting gifts waiting for you.

Always remember that God has greater things in store for you than you can ever imagine. He wants higher things for you than you want for yourself. He can do far more than we can *even ask or think.*

Believe Him and accept His call today to become one of His twentieth century prophetic voices.

And Samuel grew, and the Lord was with him, and did let none of his words fall to the ground. And all Israel from Dan even to Beersheba knew that Samuel was established to be a prophet of the Lord. And the Lord appeared again in Shiloh: for the Lord revealed himself to Samuel in Shiloh by the word of the Lord. And the word of Samuel came to all Israel.

1 Samuel 3:19-4:1

Calvary Pentecostal Camp
Ashland, Virginia

10 1/2 weeks of SPIRITUAL FEASTING every
summer, with dynamic speakers each week

Campmeeting begins the last Friday of June and
continues daily through Labor Day, with:

3 Great Services Daily: 11 AM, 3 PM and 8 PM

Special Youth Activities: 9 AM and 7 PM

For more information, write us at:

11352 Heflin Lane
Ashland, VA 23005-9707

or call:

(804) 798-7756

Come and meet God at the camp!